THE MENTAL TOUGHNESS BLUEPRINT

A GUIDE TO CHANGING YOUR MINDSET, MASTERING YOUR EMOTIONS, AND OVERCOMING CHALLENGES LIKE A PRO!

JED WOOD

CONTENTS

Special Offer	v
Introduction	vii
1. Building Mental Muscle	1
2. It's All In Your Mindset	10
3. Your Daily Mental Exercise	20
4. Making Habits Stick	29
5. Identify Your Strengths	35
6. Embrace Change	45
7. Riding the Emotional Wave	54
8. Navigating Relationships	62
9. Money Mentality	67
10. Be in the Business of Success	74
11. Quieting Your Inner Critic	80
12. Persevering Despite It All	88
Conclusion	95
A SHORT MESSAGE FROM THE AUTHOR	97
Special Offer	99
References	101

Copyright © 2021 Jed Wood. All rights reserved.

The content contained within this book may not be reproduced, duplicated, or transmitted without direct written permission from the author or the publisher.

Under no circumstances will any blame or legal responsibility be held against the publisher, or author, for any damages, reparation, or monetary loss due to the information contained within this book, either directly or indirectly.

Legal Notice:

This book is copyright protected. It is only for personal use. You cannot amend, distribute, sell, use, quote, or paraphrase any part, or the content within this book, without the consent of the author or publisher.

Disclaimer Notice:

Please note the information contained within this document is for educational and entertainment purposes only. All effort has been executed to present accurate, up-to-date, reliable, complete information. No warranties of any kind are declared or implied. Readers acknowledge that the author is not engaged in the rendering of legal, financial, medical, or professional advice. The content within this book has been derived from various sources. Please consult a licensed professional before attempting any techniques outlined in this book.

By reading this document, the reader agrees that under no circumstances is the author responsible for any losses, direct or indirect, that are incurred as a result of the use of the information contained within this document, including, but not limited to, errors, omissions, or inaccuracies.

SPECIAL OFFER

Special Bonus!
Want This Bonus Book For Free?

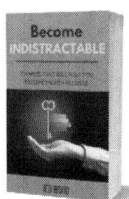

Get **FREE**, unlimited access to it and all of my new books by joining the Fan Base!

Scan With Your Phone Camera To Join!

INTRODUCTION

You begin your march to the grave the minute you take your first breath. It is fate. It is unavoidable. Everyone comes out dead on this one. But if you think this is grim news, you have not been paying attention. Mahatma Gandhi lived in the 1900s. The lawyer turned social activist was known for his compassion and his fight against British colonial rule. He made a difference in his time. He is dead. Florence Nightingale, the war-hero nurse, was a woman genuinely dedicated to helping others. When she first arrived in the army, the doctors wanted nothing to do with her, but she wouldn't go away. Nightingale was committed to doing good, and she prevailed. She is dead.

All through history, people have been dying and will continue to die as long as humanity exists. The big question is whether we will remember you when you are dead. The men and women we remember are gone, but their legacy speaks. Past the difficulties of their time, they succeeded. They didn't just survive, they excelled, and everyone around them was better for it. What did they have that you do not have? Stamina. Grit. Perseverance. Whatever the name you call it, mental toughness is undoubtedly desired and missing among many.

Think about Karen for a minute. Karen works in mid-level management in a debt collection agency. She makes enough to live on, but she has to save for longer to afford to go on a vacation or make a huge purchase, but that's not a big bother for her. She realizes that you have to start somewhere, and her starting position is better than most. That is until she logs into social media. On Facebook, Karen scrolls through her timeline and notices how well her schoolmates are doing. At 30, she thought she would be doing better. She thought she would at least afford to live in her own house and would probably be married.

There is a reason Karen shies away from relationships. Whenever she meets someone she likes enough to want to go out with, she runs away at the first sign of conflict. Karen retreats into her shell and gives excuses like how busy she is at work – far too busy to balance a relationship, too. The truth, though, is that she feels fragile. She fears that her heart would break and she would never recover. But relationships are not the only area Karen feels ill-equipped. Once, she confided in a friend that she desired a promotion. A position was open in her workplace that she knew she would have been perfect for. Her friend advised her to let her boss know that she was interested in interviewing for the job. It sounded like an excellent idea.

That night, Karen went on a mission. She would write the best 'registration of interest' email her boss had ever received. She would present her strengths and let him know why she would be a good fit. After all, she had been doing the work that she would be doing in that position for a long time, but without the official title and the pay raise that comes with it. So, she wrote and rewrote her email. She tried to edit her CV, but the morning found her having made no progress. Eventually, after many excuses and pep talks to herself, Karen decided that she would apply for it the next time it would open up. So, what was Karen's problem? A lack of mental strength.

Perhaps you, like Karen, are afraid to speak up and rock the proverbial boat. Maybe you are in a relationship that is not everything it could be. You think that if you spoke up a little bit more if you let your partner know how they could meet your needs, you would be happier. But you have no idea how to get started. Maybe, for you, the problem is the stress you feel. You are constantly apprehensive about work, afraid that you may be asked to do a task that you cannot handle. You wouldn't want to make a fool of yourself. This fear overflows into your social life, and you struggle to assert yourself. So, you let others push you around. You constantly indulge their wishes and forget to have your own needs met. You are tired of putting yourself on the backburner and desire to feel more in control of your life. You want to learn how to establish healthy habits and control your thoughts rather than be at their mercy.

If that sounds like you, this book is for you. Here, you will learn how to keep your head above water no matter what situation you find yourself in. It may be true that you become a candidate for death when you take your first breath, but it is also true that you take your first step steeped in potential. You could be one of the greats. You could live the kind of life you envision for yourself. In this book, you will learn how to get out of life alive to the grave. By this, I mean you will unlock the secret to living through every challenge life throws at you, excelling even, because you will become as solid a person as they come.

Imagine a life where you control your emotions rather than let them control you. Imagine gleaning the message they are passing and acting on it without being reactive and impulsive. Imagine participating only in the things that align with who you are and not going along with other people's plans because you are afraid to say no. How freeing would that be? You could finally develop some consistency in your efforts to make your life better. You could set up a mode of being that is fulfilling for you in the present and the future and suitable for those around you.

Think about what life would be like if your mind were not constantly committing mutiny – if your negative self-talk did not drive you to self-sabotage. How would you change the world if you were not given to expecting the worst, so much so that you make it a self-fulfilling prophecy? You would know that even if you failed, you could get back up, and, armed with a new lesson, you could try again without the self-blame and shame you often feel. Self-pity would be a thing of the past. You would finally be able to silence your inner critic. That is the promise of this book.

You will learn how to overcome your workplace and relationship challenges to no longer live under stress. You will gain confidence in your ability to achieve anything you set your mind to, which is the essence of mental toughness. I will provide you with actionable steps that you can take in your personal, social, emotional, and financial life to make it as you would have it. Consider this a mindset reset book. You get to develop habits that stick based on your strengths. You learn how to use them to your advantage and improve your weaknesses so that they do not give you an undue disadvantage.

In my time as a fitness instructor, I have seen all kinds of people come and go. Some people come to me wanting to lose weight. They only want a slim waist or more toned arms. I let them know that weight loss and fitness are not a buffet. You do not get to pick what parts of your body you want to shape and which ones stay as they are. They do not like this news. They walk away, unwilling to take a chance on themselves. Another group of people comes in and set their minds to do what needs doing. You ask them to do squats; they ask how many. You require them to adjust their diet; they are quick to oblige. These are the people who see the results. They are the ones who reap the benefits of change.

Life is a lot like exercise. You have to be willing to go all in. This book will help you build your confidence and take charge of your life only if you go all in. I know that to be true based on my over 20 years of experience as a life coach. I want to help you become mentally strong because I have seen firsthand how the right mindset and action can change a life. I learned the value of mental strength, and I have watched others acquire it and become better for it. Many years back, I unexpectedly lost my job and nearly fell into financial ruin. I was already in debt, and now I had no way to make my payments. At first, it seemed like this would be the end, but I was able to draw on the experiences and strategies I discuss in this book to navigate life despite the pressures. Eventually, I recovered and started my own business as a life coach. This happened because I refused to let the crisis define me. I exercised mental toughness and refused to give in. Here, you learn how to go through challenges without letting them destroy you, so gear up. It is time to go to war with yourself and learn how to prevail.

1

BUILDING MENTAL MUSCLE

'There is no other way to reduce the difficulty of your life than to increase the strength of your mind.' – **Mokokoma Mokhonoana.**

Have you ever considered what makes a good athlete? What do they have that causes them to stand out? What about a good leader or a good parent? Why do some people set goals, go after them, and achieve them while others are content to stay complacent? What makes the difference? Most of the time that this question is answered, people talk about talent. They might say of an athlete that they are faster than anyone else or of a leader that they are excellent at forming strategies, but there is always more to the story. As research has found, intelligence and talent, while they play a role in success, are not as influential as one may think. Intelligence accounts for only 30% of what you achieve – and that is the upper limit.

Mental toughness makes a more significant impact on a life well lived than intelligence or talent. It plays a bigger role in fulfilling your life, business, and health goals than anything else, and that is good news. It is good news because you do not need to have the right genes to get in shape or to excel at your workplace. You can simply do what you must to shape your mental toughness. In this chapter, we will discuss what mental toughness is and how it differs from resilience. Then, we will look at the components of mental toughness, and at the end of the chapter, you will find activities that you can begin to implement to build your mental strength. Before explaining precisely what it is, let us discuss why it is crucial.

WHY MENTAL TOUGHNESS MATTERS

Every year in the US, over a thousand cadets join the military academy. During their early days, they must endure brutal tests that are deliberately engineered to challenge them to the limits of their mental, emotional and physical capacities. You may expect that only the biggest, strongest, and most intelligent will complete the tests successfully, but that was not the case out of 2441 cadets involved in a recent study. The ones who finished the tests well did so on account of their passion and perseverance. It was mental toughness that caused them to succeed. This is why mental toughness is essential.

A student may not be the smartest, but they would exceed their more intelligent peers if they are mentally tough. Two people of the same age and qualifications competing for a job will be differentiated based on their mental toughness. Even in competitions that may seem trivial, like a spelling bee, competitors who do the best are those who are committed and persistent in their practice. You need to be mentally tough to do well, even in professions like law, investment banking, and medicine. Sustained commitment will win every time.

This is not just true in research environments. Think about your life for a minute; who are the most successful people around you? Is the trend true even with your past experiences? The chances are that you know an extremely talented person who squandered their gifts and cheated themselves out of many opportunities. You also likely know people who have achieved their goals regardless of the obstacles they met. These are the people who inspire us. They inspire us because of their mental toughness, and that is the bottom line.

MENTAL TOUGHNESS VERSUS RESILIENCE

Negative life events, crises, challenges, and stressors are an unavoidable part of life. Just like a rollercoaster, life has ups and downs-- some of them you can see coming, while others are an unpleasant shock that leaves you feeling blindsided. The Merriam-Webster dictionary defines adversity as "a state or instance of serious or continued difficulty or misfortune." We have all faced problems in our lives, to varying degrees. Some people are familiar with intense loss and despair, while others may not have experienced anything quite so devastating. Regardless of your life experience, you're sure to have found yourself in a situation where things seemed hopeless or downright overwhelming.

Think of a time in your life where you faced adversity. What was the event or situation that negatively affected you? How did you respond at the time? Would you choose to act differently if you had the chance?

Negative situations can have life-altering impacts on our social and mental health, especially when they aren't handled correctly. But research shows that the degree to which these experiences affect us varies from person to person. How can that be so? The answer lies in resilience, which is often confused with mental toughness, although they are not the same. Resilience is the determining factor in how people recover from and face complex life events.

Psychologists define resilience as the process of adapting well in the face of adversity, trauma, tragedy, or stress. It does not just involve "bouncing back" from these situations but also includes the personal growth required to navigate them. Certain factors might make one person more resilient than others, but it isn't a personality trait. In fact, it's a characteristic that can be developed and honed with practice and application. Essentially, you can learn resilience.

Imagine yourself going fishing in a river. You know the parts where the water is slow and raft down the river in search of these. Along with the shallows and slow water, you have a map that lets you know when you are approaching rapids. How do you make sure you pass the rough waters safely? Maybe you would freak out a little, but remind yourself to calm down. Perhaps you would automatically resort to your go-to stress response. How you handle it, is informed by your resilience. Resilience is not about removing the difficulty or avoiding the source of distress, but about coming out victorious. It is about adapting well, and it is a significant component that contributes to a person's overall wellbeing. But what about preparing for adversity in advance? What about the mental skills that you need to employ to overcome challenges? That's where mental toughness comes in.

THE CONCEPT OF MENTAL TOUGHNESS

In the raft example, while resilience is what you do when you are in the thick of things, mental toughness is what you do before. How do you fortify yourself to handle the expected rapids? Maybe you would get someone else to help you. Perhaps you would wear your life jacket, or maybe, you would confirm that you have the right tools. Whatever the solution you pick, it equates with the role mental toughness plays in our lives.

Mental toughness first emerged as a concept in sports and sports psychology but is now being recognized across several different fields. One definition of mental toughness categorizes it as *a developed or natural psychological edge.* That edge *allows you to deal with the demands of life better* than other people, to *be consistent, and to keep your cool even under pressure.* Other experts have defined it as:

"The ability to resist, handle and overcome doubts, concerns, worries, and circumstances standing in the way of success, or an objective that you set out to achieve."

Let's break that down a little. First, it's important to note that, like resilience, mental toughness is a "natural or developed" psychological characteristic. That means that even if you don't feel mentally tough now, you have the ability within you to become stronger. It is mental toughness that enables you to cope with the demands of everyday life and overcome circumstances that would otherwise hold you back or throw you off track. It helps you overcome the challenges that prevent you from succeeding, reaching your goals, and achieving all that you're capable of. It's the quality that enables you to power through a final set of reps at the gym or allows athletes to push past exhaustion to succeed.

THE CORE COMPONENTS OF MENTAL TOUGHNESS

What does mental toughness really look like in practice? How can you identify it in the real world? The following are the key components of mental toughness:

- **Consistency**

Consistency is about behaving in ways that match your past decisions. It is a form of ordered decision-making so that you do not have to make a new choice every time you meet a problem. It makes you a bit predictable, but it ensures that you thrive under challenges. If you behave consistently, you will feel optimistic about your decisions and will more likely identify a mistake when you make it. It is about concentrated attention. You make your goals and then focus on them without getting distracted by concerns over what could have been. Consistency involves a commitment that causes you to stick with tasks and finish everything you start.

In practice, consistency will look like this: say you want to read one book every month for a year. Begin by choosing the books you want to read, and then read a chapter today. The idea is to accept the first commitment to your goal, no matter how small it is. From there, you want to keep reading a chapter every day. You can let other people you trust know what is happening - the internal pressure for you to keep reading the book will be greater when other people know your decision. Then, the more you read, the more you will be motivated to read. For example, after the first month, you will have finished your first book and proven to yourself that it is indeed doable, which will strengthen you to begin the next book.

- **Perseverance**

Perseverance is about your ability to pursue a passion or goal over time and to keep doing it with delight, despite any setbacks. It is about deriving pleasure in finishing what you started. It includes a level of stress mastery. To persevere, you have to manage the pressure and stress of the moment and operate without letting anxiety and fear rule you. It is moving forward despite your anxiety and fear. If you have mastered stress, it becomes a motivator to push yourself some more and do better.

Perseverance also includes failing and growing through that failure. It is about recognizing when you have made a mistake, reflecting on it, and using it as a launchpad for personal development. A persevering person does not take failure as defining. Instead, they embrace the challenges that come their way and know how to perceive them as learning opportunities which means that if they fail, they learn.

In the example of reading a book every month for a year, here is what perseverance would look like. You get to the second month and halfway through, your boss keeps giving you work that requires you to work at home. The extra work steals from your reading time and so you skip three days. On the fourth day, you have no work, but you have lost your momentum. You do not want to keep going. Perseverance will remind you of how good you felt when you finished the first book. It will associate reading with bliss rather than with drudgery. It will cause you to take joy in doing the work and not just in the result. You will go back to reading and find a way to make up for the lost time.

- **Positive mentality**

No one has mental strength who is constantly negative in their thinking. A mentally strong person has the attitude of a winner. They are confident that whatever they set their minds to do, they will succeed. They know that their best would likely be good enough because they have taken the time to grow their skills. They believe in themselves and their ability to deal with anything if they have to.

A person with a positive mentality does not play a victim. They are not eager to assign blame to anyone but themselves. Instead, they are sure that they are running their lives. They own their choices and know that they control their destiny and their lives. To take the example of reading yet again, if you have a positive mentality, you will be able to cope when extra work infringes on your private reading time.

A positive mentality will cause you to reframe the problem. Rather than getting upset at your boss, your colleagues, and everyone else involved in giving you more work, you will appreciate the good parts in the situation - may be more work means more pay, which means you can get more books that you need to read. It is also a positive mentality that will power you to negotiate with colleagues the next time they have extra work for you so that you create the time you need to read. It will enable you to advocate for yourself.

- **Preparedness**

A mentally strong person is always prepared. They are always ready for any eventuality, so they are not surprised when unexpected things happen. This enables them to be equipped to deal with challenges well. They find it easy to respond in a measured and appropriate manner rather than to be consumed by the chaos and the stress it brings. Mentally strong people have a plan. They know how they can recover from personal failure without giving in to disappointment or their inner critic.

To yet again use the reading example, preparedness will look like picking the kind of books and the exact titles you want to read beforehand. A mentally tough person will consider the things they hope to learn or the kind of books they love to read early on. They will buy them and keep them close so that they do not have to choose what to read every month. Being prepared in that manner will make it easier for them to follow through.

CHAPTER ACTIVITY: CHART YOUR WAY FORWARD

Mental toughness is like any other body muscle and needs to be worked to grow and develop. This book will equip you to identify the areas of your life where you would most benefit from mental toughness and take action to work that mental muscle. Each chapter will end with practical action steps you can take to start building your mental toughness. For now, take a moment to take stock of yourself. Get a pen and a notebook and define the specific areas where you need to be mentally tough. It might sound something like:

- Journal five minutes every day for a month
- Reading one book a month for the next year
- Get off screens by 8:30 pm every day for a fortnight
- Try one home-cooked meal every week for the rest of the year
- Finish one course on Coursera this month
- Jumping rope for five minutes every day
- Checking up on a friend once every weeks

Whatever area you identify, make sure that you are clear about it. Do not leave it undefined. Mental toughness may be an abstract concept, but it is highly connected to well-defined actions. You cannot wish your way into mental toughness. You have to act it out into being.

2

IT'S ALL IN YOUR MINDSET

'A bird sitting on a tree does not fear the branch breaking because it trusts not the branch, but its ability to fly.' – **Anonymous.**

Your mindset affects everything you do. Nothing is exempt. It touches your professional life and defines your personal life. It shapes how you socialize and how you interact with those closest to you. It even affects how you relate to yourself. Your mindset affects the dreams you have and the choices you make to pursue them. The way you view yourself, the value you assign to who you are, how you judge your potential, and the ways you determine your worth all work together to create your life. From your days as a young child, every choice you make has been determined by what you believe about yourself. Sure, parents, friends, neighbors, and teachers influence your belief by the advice and judgment they give, but ultimately, the choice of what to believe about yourself is yours to make.

Unfortunately, as we grow up, we tend to internalize the messages we heard from those around us that directly speak to who we are. We may believe someone who says to us that school is hard. We may accept someone's reaction when we tell them what we hope for even though it seems to imply that we are crazy. We may hold on to a smile of disbelief from someone we care about when we open up. When we internalize the messages we receive, we give them more weight than our own judgment of who we are. We take on the ascribed identity and make choices based on it. We believe other people's projections of who we are and in so doing, we let others tell our stories. This chapter will look into the importance of cultivating a positive mindset. You will learn the different forms of negative thinking, how to spot them and how to manage them.

MIND YOUR MINDSET

One of the core components of mental toughness is a positive mentality. Mentally tough people don't question whether they're able to succeed or achieve their goals-- they know they can. They have cultivated the belief within themselves that despite what everyone else says, they have within them a stream of endless potential that they can direct in whatever ways they desire to shape their lives. Regardless of what your goals are, it's critical that you cultivate a genuine belief in yourself and your abilities. Your belief and confidence start largely with how you talk to yourself.

Negative thinking is a common cause when it comes to self-doubt and criticism. That nagging inner critic that loves to tear you down is fueled by a consistently negative way of thinking about yourself and the world around you. If practiced consistently, negative thinking can become a habit. It is, in fact, one habit that many people engage in without even realizing it. Before delving into the types of negative self-talk, let's first define self-talk.

Self-talk is the stream of automatic thoughts that run

through your head as you go about your day. There is often a trigger which launches a stream of thought that could either be positive or negative. Note that the trigger can be external – such as overhearing two men quarreling and immediately assuming you are in danger - or it can be internal – like remembering an event that happened in the past, which causes you to feel a certain way and triggers certain thoughts automatically.

How aware of your daily thoughts are you *really*? Do you notice the constant stream of thoughts running through your mind? If you start to pay attention, you might be surprised at what you begin to notice. Because negative thinking comes in many forms, and it can be difficult to identify at first. Here are some common forms to look out for:

WHAT STORIES ARE YOU TELLING YOURSELF?

- **Filtering**

Filtering involves making the negative aspects of a situation so big that they overshadow any positives. People who filter gloss over the positives. Twenty things could go right and they would only notice the one that backfires. Mental filtering ends up causing anxiety and depression. Here is an example of what filtering looks like in practice: Kevin is an expert web designer. He was asked to present at a workshop taking place at a local college. During the presentation, he noticed a student who walked out and never came back. After the class, many students thanked him for such a helpful presentation, but Kevin drove home angry at the one student that walked out. He believes that if the student had stayed, the lecture would have been better. Kevin is filtering.

- **Personalizing**

When you personalize, you automatically take on the blame whenever something bad happens. In personalizing, you fail to acknowledge any other factors involved in the situation. In fact, even where the situation is not connected to you, you take on the blame. An example of this negative thinking pattern is Caroline. Caroline went out with her friends for brunch at an Italian restaurant she had chosen. None of the food they ordered was up to the standard they had expected. They talked with the management and made their thoughts known before they left, but Caroline still felt that she was to blame. When the next day she saw her friends talking, she started to feel intentionally excluded. She feared that they were blaming her for the food at the restaurant. Caroline was personalizing.

- **Catastrophizing**

Catastrophizing is about automatically expecting the worst. If you are catastrophizing, you see unfavorable outcomes and decide that if they happen, life will be a disaster. For example, a student who is catastrophizing might say, 'if I fail the test tomorrow, I will never pass school and I will be a failure in life.' A person in a relationship might say something like, 'If my partner leaves me, I will never meet another person and I will never be happy.' Sometimes catastrophizing is called magnifying because you make a situation worse than it is. Essentially, catastrophizing involves predicting a negative outcome and making a conclusion that if it happens, it will result in a catastrophe. It causes you to feel helpless.

- **Polarizing**

When you are polarizing, you see things only as good or bad. You are either a perfect person or you are a complete failure. When you engage in this black and white thinking, there are no shades of gray to anything. An example of polarized thinking is where you see a coworker as having been a saint until she ate your lunch, and now you cannot even look at her. Polarized thinking causes unrealistic standards for others and yourself and certainly affects how you relate with others.

- **Fortune-telling**

Fortune-telling is about predicting the future on little or no evidence and assuming the worst-case scenario. You never consider the odds of an outcome realistically and therefore you become anxious and depressed. Note that to function as an adult is to make some sort of predictions all the time, but that is not fortune-telling. If you expect that by drinking foul-smelling milk you will get sick, you are not fortune-telling. Fortune-telling is more than making an educated guess. Applying for a job while thinking that 'I am not going to get the job,' is fortune-telling. It does not consider any evidence – in this case, your skills, what the employer is looking for, other applicants, and so forth.

- **Should statements**

'Should' statements are a thinking pattern where you put pressure and unreasonable demands on yourself which makes you feel guilty. They create a sense of failure and frustration by implying that you should, must, or ought to know more than you do. For example, Lori is afraid of flying. She has had that fear since she was young. Now, her job requires that she fly a number of times every year. When on a plane, she uses relaxation techniques and prescribed medicine to get through but recently, she noticed that her fear was getting worse. She now gets anxious days before she has a flight to catch and sometimes gets panic attacks. Instead of positively affirming herself, Lori tells herself things like, 'I must overcome this fear,' 'I should be able to do this by now.' These 'should' statements end up compounding her stress and creating a sense of disappointment, making her feel like she failed for being nervous.

CHAPTER ACTIVITY: THINK RIGHT, ACT RIGHT

Negative self-talk is essentially a trick your mind plays on you to convince you of something that is not factual. It is a ruse that you can fall into without knowing, but that once you recognize, you can overcome. The answer lies in practicing positive thinking. Practicing positive thinking doesn't mean you have to try and ignore unpleasant situations and pretend everything is fine all of the time. As a matter of fact, that would go against the mental toughness component of preparedness-- you can't be prepared for things you deliberately ignore. Instead, positive thinking involves approaching challenges and setbacks in a positive and productive way. Remember, failure is simply another way to grow, and challenges are opportunities, not obstacles. Here are some things you can do to begin to think right:

1. **Find the areas to change**

In your journal, brainstorm and identify areas of your life that you usually think negatively about. You may want to start with a broad topic, such as work, then hone in on exactly what aspects you think negatively about. Once you have some areas listed, choose one area that you can begin approaching positively and imagine what life would look like if you were successful in that one area. How would it change your relationships? Make sure to identify the specific negative thinking patterns you are prone to.

1. **Challenge your specific negative thinking patterns**

As you were identifying the areas of your life that need change, you likely started to recognize the particular negative thinking patterns that you are prone to. Here is how to deal with them:

- **Filtering** – If you are prone to filtering, remind yourself of the positives about a specific situation. Take pride in your accomplishments. When thoughts about the negatives in a specific event seem to take hold, evaluate them and let them go. In Kevin's case, to deal with his filtering, he can remind himself that he worked hard and was prepared for the workshop. He could concentrate on the positive feedback he got to create a positive outlook.
- **Catastrophizing** – If you catastrophize, take the event in question for what it is. Do not make anything more of it. If you fear you will fail your exams, rather than thinking 'I will then never leave school and will fail in life,' think 'but if I fail, I will work hard and learn from that.' Focus on the positive things that you can do – listen to music you find relaxing or take a walk. Engaging in something you enjoy will keep your mind from dwelling on the possibilities.
- **Fortune-telling** - If you find yourself fortune-

telling, think before concluding. Step back and ask yourself what you know to be true. What evidence is there that your prediction is true? Imagine you were in a court of law and you had to defend the thought you just had. What would be the evidence against it? Come up with as many reasons as you can that the conclusion/thought you had is not true. Once you prove to yourself that the thought you have is not fact, then focus on the things you know for sure. You will find that you no longer believe in fortune-telling as much. From there, when you notice the temptation to negatively predict your future, remind yourself of the possibilities for it. Bring to your mind alternative, more positive outcomes besides the one your mind is tempted to cling to. It will help you to bring you to a near-neutral position.

- **All or nothing thinking** - Avoid putting yourself in a box. Words like 'never,' 'always' or 'every' are not just negative, but they also damage your self-esteem. Think of times when these words were untrue. Rather than saying 'My coworker always eats my lunch. She is not a good person,' say instead, 'My coworker ate my lunch yesterday. It was probably by mistake.' Finding the exceptions to the rule will keep you from polarizing.
- **Personalization** - If you catch yourself personalizing, intentionally choose to think logically – it will stop you from taking full responsibility. Carefully evaluate the situation to find where your responsibility for the outcome was. Do not shoulder unnecessary blame for the responsibility or action of others.
- **Should statements** - Challenge 'should statements'

by rewording how you talk to yourself. Rather than saying 'I should know this by now,' say 'I am learning this. It is a process and it takes time.'

1. **Stay mindful throughout the day**

Once you have identified and challenged your negative thinking, watch out how you think all through the day. Make it a habit to slow down and observe yourself. Periodically throughout the day, pause for a moment and assess what you are thinking. Are your thoughts mainly negative? What have you been focusing on, possibly without realizing it? If you recognize that you're having a negative thought, try to reinterpret it in a positive way. If this doesn't seem doable, say to yourself: "this thought isn't benefiting me right now" or a similar mantra that challenges the thought itself and then let it go.

1. **Start a gratitude journal**

A gratitude journal can help you to start thinking positive thoughts by encouraging you to focus on the good. It is how you count your blessings. Recognizing the things you are grateful for and giving thanks for them has many health benefits including improving your mental health and sleep. Besides, gratitude will lift your spirit. It will make you feel happier and give you a sense of connectedness to the things you are grateful for. Challenge yourself to write in a gratitude journal for 15 minutes per day, at least once per week for the next four weeks. Make sure to always write up to five things you feel grateful for.

When journaling, remember that there is no right and

wrong way to journal. You can list even the things you judge to be of small importance as long as they give you joy. Make sure to be as specific as you can and go in-depth. Elaborate as many details as you need to, to foster a sense of gratitude. While at it, get personal – rather than saying 'I am grateful for kind people in the world,' say 'I am grateful for Chris when he was kind to me by…' (state the exact thing Chris did that convinced you of his kindness). The more specific and personal you are, the more real your feelings of gratitude will be and the longer they will last.

3

YOUR DAILY MENTAL EXERCISE

"We are what we repeatedly do. Excellence, then, is not an act, but a habit." - **Will Durant.**

When I was working as a fitness instructor, I met many people who would confess to having been motivated to work out all day, except for the few minutes leading to their time at the gym. People always ask; why does my motivation seem fickle? And the answer is always the same – you are not lacking motivation; you have bad habits. Of course, many people did not love hearing this. Some of them continued to blame their lack of motivation for a lot of their issues. They never seemed to be driven enough to do what they actually wanted to do. But there are a few people who got it. The ones who got it learned how to use their motivation to build strong and sustainable habits. They began working to get rid of their bad habits by getting rid of their cues and replacing them with positive habits. Naturally, they started to see results that drove them to work harder.

You may be like the first group of people, failing to see

how your habits are in your way, but what you do not realize is that by virtue of being human, you are bound to have many automatic behaviors, some of which are bad. This chapter is about shaping your habits. It is about consistency – an essential part of mental toughness. You will learn why identity matters if you will build mental toughness and will get to develop habits based on your identity.

CONSISTENCY, NOT MOTIVATION

A common question people ask regarding mental toughness is what aspect is the most important. Some people imagine it is willpower. Others guess motivation and a third group supposes that it is inspiration. Yet, it is neither of the three. Mental toughness is about your continued efforts, not your motivation, inspiration, or willpower. We often believe that feeling motivated to do something is the best way to accomplish it. When we feel motivated to complete a task or reach a goal, it's easier to take action and get started. But motivation, as you have probably noticed, inevitably fades.

Willpower, on the other hand, can be practiced more easily than motivation, but even that comes and goes. Our willpower can be affected easily by sleep, mood, hunger, and many more factors that interfere with our ability to exercise self-discipline. How easy do you find it to work out when you are sleepy? How easy is it to read when you are hungry? Willpower is easily overcome by life situations. Even inspiration, while helpful in creating motivation, comes and goes. You've probably been inspired by the successes of many people who you admire, but did that help you to emulate them?

What really matters to doing things in the long-term is *consistency*. Mentally tough individuals aren't set apart by their talent, intelligence, or natural abilities - they draw their power from being consistent. They have systems and attitudes that work to help them focus on their priorities regardless of obstacles or challenges. They're usually prepared for the expected and the unexpected, and their habits "form the foundation of their mental beliefs and ultimately set them apart." Mentally tough people can continue with their habits and routines even in the face of obstacles and challenges. They don't second guess themselves or question whether to keep going, they just do.

YOU ARE WHAT YOU DO

Take some time to reflect on yourself. Think about the different ways you define yourself. What are you good at? What do you do consistently, and how does it define you? While at it, figure out some of the habits you have that *aren't* serving you or supporting your ideal self. How do they contribute to your sense of identity?

To build good habits, you have to tap into the self-belief that was discussed in Chapter 2. You have to believe new things about yourself and create habits based on your identity. Having a strong sense of identity makes it much easier for you to stay consistent and make choices that are in your best interest. As you do this exercise, find your reason – what is it that gives meaning to your life? What drives you to get out of bed each day? What goals are you aiming for?

Resilient people have goals and aims that they are fully committed to. They have a reason to get out of bed in the morning and know their "why". When developing new mental habits, they don't have to rely on fleeting motivation because they see the bigger picture. If you find that you are struggling to come up with concrete answers, take some time and think about what has motivated you in the past. When did things change, and why?

FIVE THINGS MENTALLY TOUGH PEOPLE DO

Understanding characteristics that are true of all mentally tough people despite their age, status, career, race, or gender will help you to know the kind of person you are working to become. It will form a foundation for defining your goals and will help you to identify when you are close to becoming mentally tough. Mentally strong people:

1. **Focus on the things they can control**

There is a brutal truth that some people have trouble accepting – you have zero control over many things in life. People who resist this truth tend to become control freaks. They give in to micromanaging and refuse to delegate. They are always trying to get others to change because they think that if they can control others and their situations, they can prevent disaster. Other people know that they can't prevent trouble but keep worrying about it anyway. They fret even over natural disasters and pandemics, which keeps them so occupied but does them no good.

Mentally strong people do neither. They do not waste their time and effort worrying over the things they cannot control or trying to control things outside of their influence. Instead, they find what they can control. They look at life through a measured lens and when they spot a storm brewing, they quickly do what is within their control to do and leave everything else. They know that they cannot control other people's behavior, but how they respond to it. Mentally strong people understand that sometimes all that they can control is their effort and their attitude.

Mentally strong people not only remove their focus from things beyond their control, they are also alive to the fact that there are things and people they can influence. They concentrate on changing their behavior and becoming role models in their spheres of influence. They also set healthy boundaries for themselves. When their fears threaten to overwhelm, rather than predict catastrophe, they busy themselves doing what needs to be done to avoid disaster.

1. **Are comfortable being uncomfortable**

The ability to handle adversity is not just about keeping at it or crossing your fingers and wishing it away. Mentally tough people know this and have learned how to embrace challenges as opportunities for them to expand beyond their comfort zone. They are secure in the knowledge that the path to being better is paved with the challenges they overcome. Rather than run from problems or bury their heads in the sand, they charge into battle. Because of this, they gain influence over others and experience the growth that can only come from dealing with challenges.

Somewhere in the deep ocean, there is a cluster of oysters clinging to a reef. The unrelenting ocean current stirs up the seafloor and carries sand and other sediments to the oysters. As the sand and sediment pass, a speck is lodged inside one of the oysters. The speck is an intruder; an unpleasant, uncomfortable, and foreign irritant – a challenge the oyster must deal with. With time, it makes the most of the challenge and produces from it a beautiful pearl. The story of the oyster is the story of a mentally tough person. They know that without the discomfort, they have no pearls.

The mentally strong person trusts that challenges will help them to know their strengths. Nothing will help you discover what you are made of than having to handle a situation you did not expect. For the mentally strong, challenges are an opportunity to develop resilience and learn how to master their emotions. They learn how to move through sadness, anger, frustration, desperation, relief, anguish, and the many emotions they experience through the obstacles they meet. They emerge as people who can rule their emotions, which brings us to the third point.

1. **Practice emotional intelligence**

Mentally strong people are emotionally intelligent. Because of how they have learned to deal with their emotions, they can deal with other people. They know how to interpret their emotional experiences and deal with their negative emotions without resorting to destructive habits. Mentally strong people do not ignore or deny their emotions as that would only escalate them. They instead acknowledge how they feel, why, and what they can do to remedy it. They have learned their triggers and are always self-aware enough to stop themselves before they react to their emotions in a way that harms others.

The mentally strong have also honed their capacity for compassion and empathy. They can help other people to label their emotions correctly and can allow them the space they need to process how they feel. Mentally strong people try to see the world through the eyes of the people they are trying to help. They are also careful to acknowledge how their actions, ideas, and words affect others.

1. **They embrace change**

Change is inevitable. Some people have gone on to say that change is the only constant in this world. If you want to be mentally strong, you must learn to embrace the fact that nothing stays the same. You have to roll with the punches otherwise, change will overwhelm you. The mentally strong have made peace with the fact that change comes whether they want it or not and so, rather than get stuck in denial, they plan for the eventualities. They know the importance of having habits, but they never drive their security from them, but from their values – something which helps them to take the change in stride.

Mentally tough people are open to learning new things. They cultivate in themselves an attitude of accepting whatever happens and know that they can integrate change without fear. Mentally tough people know that they can master any new skills they need because something has changed. They trust that because they allow change into their lives, they become fearless, wiser, positive, and adaptive.

1. See failure as a motivator

Everyone fails at things in their life, and the fear of failure can be debilitating for people. We're all only human, and falling short of our goals is an unavoidable experience, but mentally tough people do not tap out because they fail. True, they may find failure unpleasant, but on a deeper level, they know it to be beneficial for their future. They realize that because they failed, they have a story to tell. That way, their failure can inspire others when they finally prevail. Also, mentally tough people are motivated by failure because they think of it as an opportunity to learn.

When people become successful, we often forget their failures. It is easy to imagine that someone like Oprah Winfrey has never failed, but her story is paved with many failures. Her first job was helping out at a small station. When she was hired by a television station to read the news, she thought she had her big break, but she was wrong. She failed many times before she finally succeeded. Her story is the story of every mentally tough individual – they fail, but they put their failure behind them.

CHAPTER ACTIVITY: WHO ARE YOU?

1. **Determine where you are**

The things you do are a mirror image of the type of person you believe that you are. In a journal, make a list of truths and beliefs that you have about yourself, both good and bad. Be honest and objective - don't blame or shame yourself, but try and write as many aspects of yourself as you can. If it helps, divide your life into sections and think about each individually – how do you behave at work? What do you love to do when you are alone? What is your social life like? If someone else were to describe you, what would they say? Make sure to map out as many details as you can.

1. **Decide where you want to be**

Now that you've identified where you are, you can begin to think about where you want to be. What kind of person would you rather be? If you could live your life and live it well, what would it look like? Reflect on the following questions:

- What do you want to stand for?
- What are your principles and values?
- What attributes make your ideal self?
- How is your ideal self consistent in his/her life?

1. **Be accountable to someone else**

Staying consistent can be difficult when you're only accountable to yourself. Find someone who will support you in your journey and share your goals with them. Set up a plan to check in regularly and share your progress.

4

MAKING HABITS STICK

"Motivation is what gets you started. Habit is what keeps you going." - **Jim Ryun.**

In the previous chapter, we discussed the need to be consistent and why consistency trumps motivation, but that is not to say that motivation has no place. In this chapter, you will understand how you can use motivation to power you to form habits that will serve you. You will learn the process behind habit formation and find ways you can create a system that will help you to maintain the positive habits you create. Essentially, this chapter answers the question; 'How exactly do I become consistent? How do I make my habits stick?'

HABITS MAKE BEHAVIOR

Research shows that we use two brain networks to process our thoughts. The story network is the default network on which we do life. It is the circuitry that allows us to factor in the future and the past in our thinking about the present. It is the automatic network operational when we are not focused on a task. It is also the network responsible for our social lives – the stories we tell others about who we are and the things that have happened to us. It is the network responsible for habit formation. Habits are formed when the brain connects the things we do regularly so that what we do consistently gets into our circuitry. In the end, those things activate that part of the brain naturally. For example, if you take coffee every day as the first thing when you wake up over time, the brain learns to connect waking up with a cup of coffee. Before long, preparing that coffee becomes part of the story network. It has become a habit.

The second network is the direct experience network. It is the network responsible for how you experience whatever is happening to you through your senses. It watches what is happening outside and inside your body without any judgments. Most of us spend our time in the story network so we miss the benefits of the direct experience network. Imagine going to see the Eiffel Tower. After months of planning, you get there with your friend and the first thing you tell them is that you want to plan to come back to Paris. Do you see how ridiculous that is? You have not yet left Paris, but you are already dreaming of coming back, rather than enjoying being there. At the time you are making the comment, your direct experience network is repressed. You are not in the moment, but with some intentionality, you can change that. For the sake of clarity, the two networks are always active – you are constantly balancing between processing what is happening and creating an internal narrative, but the story network can easily create the wrong story.

People who meditate develop the ability to notice each of the networks at work in their lives. They typically can identify when they are not in the moment and recenter themselves, which means that they are better able to manage their emotions. Another research from Duke University found that over 40% of what we do is a habit, not conscious thought - the story network is certainly at play. What you may not realize is that you can rely on the direct experience network to override the story network to begin forming new habits. You can choose an action that disrupts a story you have been telling yourself and repeat it for a while to take advantage of the story network - to allow the brain to make it part of who you are. We discuss more of this in the next section, but the research implies that what you do on a regular basis makes the person you ultimately become. It also means that when you change your habits, you change your life.

HOW HABITS ARE FORMED

Have you ever asked yourself why it is so difficult to form new habits? People find it hard to form new habits because they do not know the structure of a habit, so they keep doing things that would not work, losing a game they have not started playing. Without knowing how a habit is formed, you risk shooting yourself in the foot. All habits have three components – a cue, an action, and a reward. A cue is the part of your habit where you are triggered to do something. It can come from your external or internal environment. The action is the thing you do after the trigger and the reward is the part where your brain feels rewarded after you do the desired activity. It follows that if you do not reward yourself for an action that will help you create a good habit, you are cheating yourself.

Think of it this way – the worst habits have a reward that you get without working too hard. For example, if you are in the habit of drinking, the reward is the lightness you feel when your brain is flooded with dopamine. By nature, alcohol rewards the brain and encourages you to keep drinking even though that affects your health. But, positive habits like meditation and hard work do not have obvious rewards. You receive the immediate reward of hard work after it has become a habit – then, it can stimulate your brain to produce dopamine. Before hard work is a habit, you are left with the promise of a reward at some point in the future. Do you see the problem?

The delayed reward is true for most positive habits – their impact develops over time. Meditating for only one day will not change your brain, just like one day of exercise will not alter your physique. However, if you sustain your meditative practice, it will become an activity that stimulates your brain, as will exercise. So how do you change this? One study found that associating extrinsic motivation with a positive habit can make it easier to maintain the habit. For example, you can eat dark chocolate every time you work out. Your brain starts to learn that exercise is a good thing. The point here is that if you are struggling to make and keep a habit, you may not be taking advantage of the structure of habits.

CHAPTER ACTIVITY: BUILD HABITS THAT STICK

Here are some things you can do to create and maintain healthy habits:

1. **Start small**

To strengthen your mental muscle, you have to train it every day. There are no shortcuts or cheat codes to get you there-- commitment and consistency are the keys to success. You have to build on small, daily accomplishments that push you to grow. Many people set lofty, ambitious goals for themselves without considering how realistic or practical they are. Then, when they inevitably fail, they feel discouraged and defeated which makes them even less likely to try again in the future.

1. **Get back on track quickly**

Everyone makes mistakes and gets off track, even the most mentally tough people. What sets them apart from most people is that they get back on track as quickly as they can. They do not make excuses for themselves. Remember that missing a habit once won't ruin your long-term progress, missing it continually will.

1. **Take stock**

You want to make sure that you are benefiting the most you can, from all the resources that are available to you. To do this, ask yourself these three simple questions;

- How can I incorporate cues in my environment to remind me to act?
- What are some ways I can limit the barrier to action for my habit?
- How can I reward myself positively to encourage the habits I want to keep?

For example, if the habit you want to maintain is exercising, you can decide to work out from the home to remove the barrier of having to commute to the gym and to pay a membership fee. You can make dropping your kids off at school your cue so that your brain learns that the first thing you do when you come back is to work out. Then, you can reward yourself by eating a bar of dark chocolate whenever you work out.

1. **Leave behind the all-or-nothing mentality**

No one is perfect, and expecting yourself to be able to show up each day is an easy way to become discouraged.

1. **Create a reward system**

As you now know, having a motivating reward can make it easier to stick with positive habits that don't immediately trigger our 'happy hormones'. Create a list of the habits you'd like to incorporate into your life, and see if you can identify a reward for each one. Get creative with it!

5

IDENTIFY YOUR STRENGTHS

'Don't push your weaknesses, rather, play to your strengths.' –
Jennifer Lopez.

Don Clifton, an American Psychologist, once asked a question; 'What would researchers find if they studied what is right with people instead of what is wrong with them?' At the time, he was only giving a research proposition. He couldn't have imagined his words would relate to people down the decades and how much potential they hold for change. Essentially, he was asking, if you want to improve yourself, do you work on your weaknesses or do you play to your strengths? In my years as a coach, I can certainly say that playing to your strengths is your surest bet.

In my days as a fitness instructor, before starting any workout regime with someone, I asked them to set a goal. In that process, as if it was a, by the way, I would ask them to tell me two of their biggest weaknesses. 90% of the time, they listed more than three, without skipping a bit. Some people even went on listing their weaknesses until I had to stop them. Then, I would ask them to list their strengths and they would lose all their confidence. They would hesitate and become self-conscious. If they managed to list one or two strengths, those would almost be whispered. It was baffling to me. I always wondered why people seemed shy about their strengths.

Why are most people very confident about their weaknesses but with the same measure, uncertain about their strengths? As a society, we tend to zoom in on the negative either when describing ourselves or when describing others. You step into a meeting and the manager says something like, 'let us focus on the areas we can improve...' without acknowledging where as a team, you did well. When considering a relationship, you might wonder why your potential partner, who seems so perfect, is still single. You begin to imagine that they have some major faults that they have managed to hide from the world.

The tendency to focus on the negative also means that you are likely to focus on the things you are bad at. This means that your internal dialogue is repeatedly playing your weaknesses to you. Of course, this shows up in your conversations too. The mentally strong have learned how to play to their strengths and this chapter is about that. You will learn how to use your strengths to find success in your life.

PLAY TO YOUR STRENGTHS

Everyone has unique strengths, but not everyone recognizes them or uses them to their full potential. Mentally strong people recognize their strengths and use them to their advantage to overcome challenges and reach their goals. They do not waste time and effort focusing on their weaknesses but instead streamline their progress by highlighting what they're already good at. Cultivating mental toughness is about regularly identifying your strengths in order to seek out environments where you are best suited and will thrive.

Reflection: *Think back to your life; have you ever felt stuck in a job? Have you ever been in an environment where everything you did felt draining? Perhaps you kept staying because you needed the money.*

If you examine that situation carefully, you will find that you were likely feeling underutilized – your strengths weren't being used as they could. Research has found that people who select their work based on their strengths are happier. They have lower depression levels and tend to be more energetic in their work because their mental health is in good shape.

Similar research also found that people who use their strengths at work experience less stress. They tend to be more positive which makes them lean toward kindness when the situation calls for it. They are able to self-regulate more successfully, which creates a buffer against the effects of stress. As if that is not enough, these people feel healthier and report high energy levels. They tend to be more likely to practice healthy habits like eating healthy and working out, which further endorse their strengths.

Consequently, those who use their strengths feel satisfied with their lives. They enjoy their work and feel that they are in control of their choices. It is easy for them to find workable solutions to their problems and to be more resilient when they fail. They are confident and sure of their ability to prevail no matter what they encounter. Because their attitude is positive, they grow faster as they are open to criticism and are given to self-monitoring so that they can build their strengths to meet a specific challenge. They tend to be creative at work and to be more involved than people who do not play to their strengths. In leadership positions, they end up encouraging their team to perform better. They benefit from high productivity levels within their staff, satisfied customers, and higher profits.

Yet, with all these benefits, not nearly enough people even know their strengths, to begin with. That is because recognizing strengths is not as easy as it may sound. It requires careful attention and a commitment to self-reflection, which is what the strategies provided in this chapter will help you to do. Before delving into that though, let us define strengths.

WHAT ARE YOUR STRENGTHS?

Many people assume that strengths are the same as talents, but they are not. A talent is a natural ability while strength is something you can develop and hone. For example, if you are drawn to strangers and you love the challenge of connecting with them, that is a talent. But, if you consistently build a network of supporters who are always ready to help you, that is a strength.

Strengths help you to get back on track when you fall off the wagon. When nurtured, they can help you to not only do well in your own life but to deeply impact other people's lives. Talent can take you a short distance but strengths will take you the whole way. Strengths like commitment, agility, and determination will keep you going as much as you need to. Strength is not just something that you are good at. True strength must meet the following criteria:

- You are good at it or could potentially become good at it
- Doing it energizes you
- Its benefits extend beyond yourself

In that sense, a strength is something that you can grow and expand as you challenge and exercise it. You can repeat it across time, with an impressive track record. Strengths have the biggest potential for bringing fulfillment into your life because your efforts produce the greatest results when you focus on your strengths. With that in mind, here are some concrete steps you can use to identify your strengths and begin using them:

HOW TO IDENTIFY YOUR STRENGTHS: DEVELOP SELF-AWARENESS

Growing in self-awareness offers a crucial step in knowing where your strengths lie and have major payoffs. According to research, when we see ourselves clearly, we become more creative and confident. Keep in mind though that you do not exist as an island. Your strengths work alongside other people's strengths and weaknesses, whether at work, in your communities, or at home. In becoming more self-aware, you want to understand how your strengths work alongside other people in your life and how you can make them work for you.

As a result, you must work on both external and internal self-awareness. Internal self-awareness is about seeing yourself and acknowledging your passions, reactions, thoughts, and feelings. It will help you to identify your strengths and will also improve your relationships. Growing your internal self-awareness will lower feelings of depression and anxiety. On the other hand, external self-awareness is about how other people see you, your behaviors, reactions, and strengths. The higher your sense of external self-awareness, the more empathetic you will become.

- **Listen to feedback**

Feedback can help you to build your external self-awareness. You can learn from how other people see you. They are likely to notice things in you that you didn't even see in yourself. You can begin to see who you are accurately by listening to the thoughts others have about your work and your person. Other people are one of the reliable sources you have for the things you do regularly. Make sure that you listen to the feedback of people you work with on a regular basis. When your coworkers highlight your strengths and praise your performance, pay attention to that. Think about the aspects of your work where you receive the most compliments and determine the skills or traits that allow you to do those tasks.

You can develop external self-awareness also by asking other people directly. While you can get a rough idea of your strengths by taking feedback seriously, asking your friends and colleagues direct questions may also provide additional insights. If you choose to go this way, make sure you seek opinions from different sources – a manager, friend, coworker, or even someone you oversee. If you pick people in different capacities, they will be able to give concrete examples that provide valuable context. You can make a list of your strengths in the workplace as they list them and then, later on, find the commonalities to help you compile your strengths.

Seeking out external feedback may also mean working with a mentor or a coach. There are times in life when you will need a cheerleader to help you to keep to the course. A mentor or a coach may give you the much-needed push to keep going. More importantly, they can help you to pin down your strengths and use them in your daily life. Ensure that you enlist a coach who leads by example and whose advice is practical.

While at it, be keen to surround yourself with people who

are supportive of what you are doing. The people around you can change a lot about your life. They impact your thought patterns, behavior, and self-perception. Your strengths will not be expressed or developed unless you are in an environment that is supportive, inviting, and filled with genuine people. This means that you stand to benefit if you spend your time with people who desire your success nearly as much as you do.

- **Consider your passions**

It is often much easier to develop your skills in a specific area when you enjoy what you are doing. As such, your passions may clue you in to your strengths. Think about the things you most enjoy doing. How much time do you delegate to them? Pay extra attention to those things where you lose track of time as you do them and consider the broad skills that you use while doing them. Some areas may not be natural talents, but potential places for you to grow with time and careful focus. Understanding your passions will help you to know what you are willing to give your time to until you gain expertise.

For example, if you spend a huge chunk of your downtime drawing, you may find it easy to develop creativity, attention to detail, and patience. These strengths can be used in different situations in the workplace, from teaching and administrative work to graphic design. Bear in mind the fact that if you enjoy things other people don't, that may be a strength in itself. Pursuing your interests and unique talents may provide an excellent way to identify your strengths.

While attempting to identify your strengths in this way, pay close attention to the times that you are most productive. All through your daily activities, how long does it take you to complete tasks? When are you most engaged? If you feel like time passes quickly when doing some tasks, you may be using some of your strengths. Keep a record of the times when you are most focused and the things that you find motivating during those periods. Make a note of the periods when time seems to drag by. It may show you the situations you need to avoid as you try to grow your strengths.

- **Take a personality test**

Personality tests can help you to recognize the areas where you are succeeding and your aptitude for skills and activities that you have not even tried. There are many personality tests that you can take based on the specific life area you want to examine. For example, some tests can help you to choose a career path that lines up with your interests and talents. Other personality tests focus on interpersonal strengths such as leadership styles which could prove helpful as well. You can use your results to figure out how your strengths complement other people's.

- **Seek out new experiences**

Growing your self-awareness will hugely depend on your experiences in life and so you stand to benefit from trying new hobbies, skills, and activities. In the workplace, be sure to seek out opportunities for professional development. Take risks by agreeing to collaborations outside of your regular skillset. You can also take classes to learn things you didn't know. You can shadow your boss on a networking event or you can ask coworkers to teach you a new technical skill. The idea is to step out of your comfort zone. You may be surprised to discover strengths you did not even imagine possible.

DIFFERENTIATE BETWEEN PSEUDO AND TRUE STRENGTHS

While trying to identify your strengths, be careful about pseudo strengths. A pseudo strength appears to be a strength from the eyes of onlookers but is draining from inside. They are things that you can do better than most people but when you have completed them, you feel drained. Simply because you excel at something does not mean that you will enjoy doing it. There are times when your strengths may not align with your personality. For example, you could be excellent at networking, but also an introvert, in which case networking will leave you weaker, not stronger.

Be careful of the conflict between being the most productive and feeling your best. Consider your strengths and where they overlap with your personality and your passions. This will require more time and self-reflection. Ask yourself what you feel when you employ a particular strength. Do you feel empowered and energized or exhausted and empty? You will end up burned out if you pursue strengths that do not align with your personality. The idea is to find the sweet spot between your passions, strengths, and personality.

CHAPTER ACTIVITY: FIND YOUR STRENGTHS

1. **Write down your strengths**

Take some time to reflect on this chapter and to attempt some of the strategies to identify your strengths. Figure out the things you enjoy and the skills they involve. What makes you feel valued? Make a list of your strengths, doing your best to stay as objective as you can, and be honest with yourself.

Once you've completed this list, ask a close friend what they would say your strengths are. You can even run your list by them. Ask up to ten people who know you well to write down three times they witnessed you at your best. Try to ask a diverse group, including mentors, peers, and family members.

1. **Take a personality test**

Afterward, take a personality test. You can consider any one of the following:

- The VIA character strengths inventory - a short questionnaire based on 24 character strengths.
- The Big Five Personality test - a free test that scores you on the 5 personality traits of openness, conscientiousness, extraversion, agreeableness, and neuroticism.

1. **Reflect on the result to find your best self**

With the results of the personality test, other people's feedback, and your self-assessment, identify the patterns that cut across. What themes can you identify and what strengths do they suggest? Outline what you're best at according to others, and pick out the things that you also enjoy doing. Those represent your strengths almost accurately. Experiment with them through different life experiences and be sure to come back to the list to make adjustments as necessary.

6

EMBRACE CHANGE

'The only thing that is constant is change.' – **Heraclitus.**

Many people fear it, but the reality is that change is a part of life whether you want it to be or not. With the right attitude, the change allows you to grow, which is something mentally tough people are constantly striving to do. Mentally tough people have made peace with the fact that change is inevitable. Sometimes you will see the change from around the corner and will know how to prepare for it. Other times, change will find you when you are unprepared. Whatever the case, the sooner you embrace the unknown, the sooner you can start to take advantage of your new situation.

__Reflection__: Think of a time when you experienced an unexpected change in your life. How did it feel at the moment? How did you react to the situation? How did you grow from the experience?

If I am being honest, I never really have problems with change. I welcome it with open arms. But that wasn't always the case. When I was struggling to get my finances and my life together, some days were so hard that the only thing that kept me going was the knowledge that someday, things would be different. In the depths of struggle, and without being aware of it at the time, change became a salve to me. I started to see it as a joyous thing - to remain stagnant is like death. You can accomplish nothing if you do not move forward. This chapter focuses on the importance of adapting to and embracing change when it occurs. It provides advice on how to become better at dealing with change, and how to practice acceptance.

CHANGE MUST COME

In life and work, change must come if you will grow as a person. You have to yield to it so that when faced with new situations, you are challenged to evolve. Change is not easy or natural, but it is inevitable. For most people, the natural response to change is to go back to their comfort zone – they drift toward the safety of normalcy, and understandably so. No one enjoys living with the possibility that they may be hurt. Yet, developing mental strength is about accepting change and allowing it to shape your development.

Since most people run away from change, they go through their lives without ever living up to their potential and fully expressing who they are. They never quite understand that change is happening all around us. People are forever aging, changing, and expanding. Life forms around you are always evolving. The world is not at stasis. So, to close your eyes to change is to deny yourself of something that makes you integrally human. The best approach is to let change work for you and to benefit you. That way, you are happier with your life, and the growth process. To learn to embrace change, you have to come to terms with some truths:

- Sometimes we bring change about - There are times we change because we are dissatisfied with our lives. While difficult, this type of change is the easiest for most people to embrace.
- You can create change before it happens to you – Initiating change will always be easier because you use your free will. Otherwise, when change happens to you, its effects could be dramatic and difficult to recover from.
- Your attitude counts more than you know – How you see life affects your ability to embrace change. If you handle change with a relaxed and calm mind, you are more likely to find it easier to deal with.
- It is normal to deal with uncertainty and fear – Everyone battles with this in the face of change. The mentally tough proceed despite being afraid and unsure.
- Self-loathing will never move you forward – Often, when change is unexpected, or when they inadvertently trigger change, people resort to self-loathing. They cave into self-pity which makes them counterproductive. Never blame your environment for change. Keep focused; it will help you to embrace change.

Simply put, wherever you are in life, change must come. The important thing is to value the journey change takes you through. Make peace with the fact that anything worth doing takes time, then practice acceptance when change comes your way.

PRACTICING ACCEPTANCE

It is easy to fall apart, become helpless and give up in the face of an unexpected negative change. One might even be excused for responding that way given that tragedy disempowers. Other people find it easier to deny their circumstances. Rather than face the calamity, they bury their heads in the proverbial sand. The idea of change is that life fails to go according to plan- situations fail to work out or you are part of unexpected negative experiences. In such cases, your attitude matters more than much else.

Some years ago, I lost a dear friend to terminal cancer. During that period, I had just moved to a new neighborhood to try and control my expenses and he was my only friend within miles. We spent a lot of time together before his diagnosis. I was there when he passed on. Watching someone you love take their last breath is one of the most gut-wrenching experiences in life. On the one hand, you are at peace that their suffering is over, but on the other hand, you are in immense pain that they are no longer physically here.

Talk about change - one morning I went from spending my evenings with a friend to spending my evenings alone, utterly devastated. Yet, that period we spent together, rekindling our friendship was one of the greatest gifts he ever gave me. It was not easy, but it solidified lessons I was learning about accepting change.

Acceptance is necessary when coming to terms with things that you cannot control. It does not mean to be complacent or to deny the effects of the change. Acceptance is about seeing things exactly the way they are. It is about finding the strength to work past your default response. It is getting over the initial shock and blow of change and making a choice. In the thick of things, mentally tough people recognize that they have a question to answer – will the challenge incapacitate you or will you rise above it and make the best of the situation?

EVALUATE YOUR LEVEL OF CONTROL

Sometimes, it is simpler to get fixated on events you cannot control as you try to get back your sense of control. That is normal, too. We like to feel in control of our lives and situations. It gives us a sense of reassurance and competence so that when that feeling is lost life gets uncomfortable.

Rather than blaming others when you encounter change though, you can focus on the things that you can actually control. Mentally tough people do not try to move the immovable. They are more concerned with taking responsibility. Rather than look for someone to lay blame on or ruminate on things that cannot change, they look for opportunities to empower themselves. They try to change what they can.

In the face of change, focus on your sphere of influence. Allow yourself to be consumed by the tasks that you can complete. It will help to shift your mindset and leave you feeling more fulfilled and happier. If a project or a situation feels overwhelming, try breaking it down into small steps that you can complete daily to make your situation better.

Reflection: If you are currently dealing with a change that is difficult to handle, consider your level of control. Ask yourself "What can I take responsibility for in this situation?" Find opportunities to empower yourself and create your own change. It will help you feel less stuck.

HOW TO GET BETTER AT DEALING WITH CHANGE

- **Accept the past, stay in the present and claim the future**

While change can't be avoided, you always have the freedom to choose how you react to it. The Austrian philosopher and psychiatrist, Victor Frankl talked a lot about this when he returned from his days in Nazi death camps. At the time, he learned that his mother, wife, brother, and child were all dead – everything he knew had changed. He lost everything he loved, but that did not dissuade him from life. Soon, he discovered that even though he could not turn back time and have everything he loved back, he could still find love again, make friends, enjoy music, father a child, and work with other people. He described his hope as 'tragic optimism.'

While Victor Frankl's story is an extreme example of change and loss, it perfectly illustrates the fact that the future does not have to be defined by the past. You can always find another thing to look forward to, rather than fixating on the limitations that follow a specific change. You can refuse to succumb to despair, worry and bitterness. You can accept change in the present and employ your freedom to design your future.

To do this, you have to root yourself in the present, however uncomfortable it may seem. You have to accept that change is mutually exclusive with stability. In the late 1970s, Salvatore Maddi, a researcher at Chicago University, started studying the concept of stability. He used employees in a phone company to conduct his research. At the time, the phone industry was regulated, causing the company the employees worked at to experience many changes. Some managers there struggled to cope, while others thrived. He wondered why and looked for reasons behind it - the two groups were separated by their expectation that stability is a hoax.

The leaders who thrived were adaptive. They looked at all changes – unwanted or wanted – as part of being human. They did not play the victim. Rather than imagining themselves unlucky, they engaged themselves in their work and identified opportunities to fix problems. On the other hand, the struggling leaders kept reminiscing about the past. They invested their energies in trying to understand why their luck had run out. They tried to return to a time that was long past and ended up miserable. In the end, Maddi concluded that to adapt well to change, you must let go of the past, stay in the present while shaping your future.

- **Talk about problems and challenges more than feelings**

Most people incorrectly assume that you cope better with change if you are able to talk about your frustrations, fears and anger. This couldn't be further from the truth. Research has proven that actively and repeatedly going through negative emotions stands in the way of the natural process to adapt. That is to say, if you keep talking about how disappointed you are that something has changed, that won't help you. And no, the point here is not that you should 'suck it up.' Rather:

- Identify your anger or anxiety toward change - admit that you are hurt by the change.
- Validate your feelings by acknowledging that the change is disorienting.
- Then, take stock of how your emotions might

distort your thinking.

Once you have dealt with your emotions, look for practical advice. Do not dwell on negative feelings. Find a way forward. It will help you to zoom in on the problems you can solve rather than keep you stuck, lamenting over what once was. You can identify practical ways to move forward by looking at the root cause of the change.

- **Focus on your values instead of your fears**

Focusing on what motivates you and the things that are important to you can create a buffer against stress and anxiety associated with unexpected change. Remind yourself of your core values. What do you find to be the most important in your relationships with your friends and family? What are your convictions about life? How would you like to be remembered when you die? Answering these questions can help you to shift your focus from problems. Reflecting on a personal value helps us take a step back from the immediate situation and recognize that despite external changes, our values and identity remain intact.

CHAPTER ACTIVITY: HANDLE CHANGE LIKE A PRO

1. **Strengthen your mind**

At least twice a week, spend 10 minutes writing about a time when a particular value you hold positively affected your life. How does that value remain constant even when you're experiencing change?

1. **Actively incorporate change into your life**

Look for one thing this week you can choose to do differently. When we get too comfortable in our routines, any change can seem catastrophic. By getting comfortable with small changes on a daily basis, you're priming your mind to be better equipped for big changes when they occur.

1. **Release your regrets**

Focusing too much on the past and how things used to be can cause you to miss out on opportunities in the present. Take 15-20 minutes to record past events or experiences that are still affecting you today. Ask yourself the following questions:

- What do I wish had gone differently?
- Why am I still holding onto this experience?
- How does it continue to affect me?
- What can I do to learn from it and move forward?

7

RIDING THE EMOTIONAL WAVE

"Building mental strength is about regulating your emotions, managing your thoughts, and behaving in a positive manner, despite your circumstances." - **Amy Morin.**

The ability to reflect on your emotions and manage your responses well is referred to as 'emotional intelligence.' This chapter tackles emotional intelligence, how it relates to mental toughness, and how to regulate your emotions in stressful situations. Here, you will learn how to ride the emotional wave.

***Reflection:** Have you ever gone through a stressful experience and later asked yourself "how could I have handled that differently?" Or do you struggle to control your emotions, whether that's anger, overwhelm, anxiety or frustration? If you do, there are practical ways you can learn from your emotions and manage how you respond.*

To be on the same page, 'riding the wave' is a term psychologists use to describe the ebbs and flows of life.

Sometimes, the waves will be big whole small at other times. The idea of 'riding the wave' is that if you can learn how to observe when the waves (emotions) start to swell and experience the associated feelings, you can mindfully ride the waves out without being swept away.

MENTAL TOUGHNESS VS. EMOTIONAL INTELLIGENCE

To develop mental toughness, you have to develop self-knowledge. It's only by recognizing the areas you want to change that you can begin the process of change. Changing is easier still if you can pinpoint how you respond to stress. That way, you will know the responses you are working to control, and that is the essence of emotional intelligence. The dictionary defines emotional intelligence as:

'Knowing how to use your emotions well and suitably in different situations while at the same time using those emotions to become more intelligent.'

By nature, some people are more emotionally intelligent than others, although everyone must watch how they interact with others. An emotionally intelligent person is self-aware. They are empathetic and can relate with others well even when there is conflict. They know how to advocate for their rights and ask for support when they need it.

Emotionally intelligent people can accurately recognize and understand emotion in themselves and others, and control their emotions to promote growth. Essentially, their thoughts and behaviors guide their emotions-- their emotions don't guide their behaviors. They are socially adaptable and aren't dominated by feelings of despair and fear.

SKILL DOMAINS OF EMOTIONAL INTELLIGENCE

To grow in emotional intelligence, you have to develop the following skill domains:

- **Self-awareness**

Self-awareness is your ability to identify and label feelings as they are happening. It involves the ability to see who you are well through introspection and reflection. While you may never become totally objective about yourself, you can grow in self-awareness because it exists on a spectrum. Theories about self-awareness are based on the idea that your thoughts do not define you. You are the person watching your thoughts – the thinker. You are apart and separate from your thoughts.

- **Emotional management**

Emotional management includes your ability to control your expression of emotions so that it remains appropriate in the context of a given situation. Emotional management is about maintaining perspective, self-soothing, and being able to overcome disproportionate reactions. It is the ability to use self-awareness constructively to handle challenging and positive emotions. It includes processing those emotions and determining a way forward.

- **Self-motivation**

Self-motivation goes a step beyond your basic motives. It is about following through on making positive changes in life without getting tired. Self-motivation requires that you believe in yourself and stay inspired despite challenges. It is your ability to drive yourself to take initiative and to pursue a course of action toward your goals. It is self-motivation that will allow you to complete tasks that otherwise appear mundane. It is the inner drive to achieve and create. It allows you to delay gratification, avoid acting impulsively and stay true to your goals no matter the emotions you are experiencing.

- **Empathy**

Empathy refers to the ability to understand other people's emotions and see things from their perspective. It has much to do with being able to emotionally walk in their shoes, feeling their feelings after them. When you see someone suffering, if you are empathetic, you are able to imagine yourself in their place and to feel sympathy for them. Generally, most people are attuned to their feelings, but they struggle to understand other people's emotions, which is why empathy must be cultivated. Empathy allows you to notice and interpret other people's needs and wants.

- **Relationship management**

Despite how it has been used within the context of businesses, relationship management is a little more than managing your image. On an individual level, it involves showing others, by your words and your conduct, that you want to engage with them meaningfully. It is about affirming them when there is a need to, correcting them and being fully present when interacting with them. Relationship management is doing everything within your power to make sure your relationships are just as beneficial to others as they are to you. More about it is discussed in the next chapter.

These five skills combine to form what translates as

emotionally intelligent behavior. As it is, people begin to work on their emotional intelligence from different weak and strong points. Some people find it easy to develop empathy and self-awareness while others struggle or even fail to see the need. Fortunately, in looking at what constitutes emotional intelligence and how much better it improves lives, you can be sparked to grow yourself in the areas of need.

CHARACTERISTICS OF EMOTIONALLY INTELLIGENT PEOPLE

For the sake of clarity, emotionally intelligent people embody the following characteristics:

- **They are effective communicators with good people skills**

Effective communicators pass their message thoroughly and are responsive to the input of others. They speak clearly and directly, using appropriate and simple language. They tend to be assertive with their perspectives and feelings, but they are open to other people's suggestions. When listening, they make eye contact and use affirming language. Because they speak honestly and listen well, other people trust them and ask them for advice.

- **They feel like they are in control of their lives**

For many people, the pace of their life has sped up to a level where they cannot adapt. They move through moments in a buzz of worry that they are not where they are supposed to be. They are forever anxious, making it hard to complete small tasks. Their daily routine includes responsibilities and activities that keep them stressed. Though unhappy, they have no idea how to change things. Emotionally intelligent people are not like that. They do not feel overwhelmed by life or struggle to make choices. They do not start their days feeling stuck or thwarted. Rather, they have agency – they can cut through everything that pulls at them and are able to think clearly. They are in command of their lives.

- **They learn from past experiences**

Emotionally intelligent people do not take mistakes casually. They are not only eager to move past the mistakes they make, but also excited about the lesson they get. They intentionally work to learn from their past experiences. They handle the things that happen to them, especially the bad experiences, with a sense of responsibility and thoughtfulness, which makes it possible for them to find the lesson.

- **They are empathetic towards other people**

The emotionally intelligent person knows that they do not exist in a vacuum. While they are careful to get their needs met, they also watch out that other people's needs are met as well. They do not look at other people's problems with apathy. They are able to see other people's emotions, acknowledge them, and help them to figure out a solution. In that sense, the emotionally intelligent person has a social conscience. They recognize the value of helping others.

CHAPTER ACTIVITY: RIDE THE WAVE

1. **Practice active listening**

Active listening is a listening pattern where you stay engaged with your conversation partner actively. When they speak, you paraphrase and reflect back on what they said, withholding advice and judgment. The other person ends up feeling heard and valued. To practice active listening:

- Make eye contact as the other person speaks
- Do not interrupt them
- Watch their facial expression and listen to their tone of voice to understand things they may leave unsaid
- Shut down any internal dialogue as you listen – do not daydream or think about what you say next
- Ask questions to clarify what is said
- Be patient and withhold judgment

1. **Practice self-management and self-awareness**

Make a habit of checking in with yourself all through the day to see how you feel. Be intentional when you encounter a negative event to ask yourself how it makes you feel. Recognizing and naming your emotions will help you to manage them well in stressful situations.

1. **Try deep breathing**

Controlling your breathing is a great way to ground yourself in stressful situations, and give yourself time to recognize your emotions before you respond. The next time you feel emotions start to take control, breathe in slowly, visualizing your breath rising from deep in your stomach. Hold your breath for a count of three, then let it out slowly.

Repeat as needed until you sense a calmness washing over you.

1. **Use a mantra**

Mantras can be very useful as a grounding exercise. Choose a phrase that calms and centers you, such as "I am relaxed" or "I manage my emotions with ease,' and repeat it to yourself whenever you feel your emotions begin to run wild.

8

NAVIGATING RELATIONSHIPS

"Each relationship nurtures a strength or weakness within you." - **Mike Murdock.**

If you have ever been at a bad place in life, maybe deep in debt, or surrounded by a lot of toxicity, you know how difficult it is to begin to make changes to get out. You are also familiar with the one thing that gives you the strength to try again even though things seem not to be working - a support system. Only after finding people who believe in you and are willing to support you, are you able to find the strength to keep trying to get better. You lean on the strength of your friends to draw out your own power. This is why relationships are important in life, and I would argue, vital.

Having a support system in place allows you to feel more confident in your abilities, take greater risks, and feel more optimistic about life overall. Yet, creating and maintaining healthy relationships is not straightforward. To do it, you have to understand how relationships work and what is expected of you as a part of the relationship dynamic. Such an understanding will help you not to take relationships for granted, and to honor all the commitments you make in relationships. This chapter will provide such understanding. It will help you to apply emotional intelligence to your relationships productively.

SOCIAL SUPPORT AND MENTAL TOUGHNESS

Whenever something tragic happens to me, the first thing I do is call my best friends. Like the good friends they are, they often drop whatever they are doing and come to help. Having them has made a difference in getting through difficulties in life. That is the value of relationships. Researchers have not always known how important social support is to a person's mental toughness. For a period, they emphasized only the place of personal qualities. According to one study, people are happier when they have meaning in their lives and when they believe they have some level of control over their lives.

Other studies suggested that it is personality factors that influence how people recover from economic hardships. They suggest that those who are conscientious have better health outcomes and a low risk of suicide. Yet, this research does not tell the whole story. Researchers discovered this only recently when they started looking at the role relationships play in a person's ability to recover from hardship and move forward productively and adaptively. They have realized that mental toughness fluctuates across time based on the environmental changes around an individual. How mentally strong you are has a lot to do with having social support – institutions, communities, and culture.

According to one researcher, the availability of social support is crucial for people in the face of challenges. People with positive relationships and a supportive environment are much more likely to prevail against challenges. It follows that having good social support is a winning life strategy connected to better physical and psychological well-being. It helps you to feel less stressed when you are suffering.

The impact of social relationships on a person's mental strength does not end at helping them prevail against obstacles. Research has also shown that positive relationships at one point in your life will make you less likely to be depressed later in life. They offer protective benefits for the elderly whose cognitive abilities may be declining in addition to having health challenges. Undoubtedly, social relationships are important for health. If you stack them against other risk factors like obesity and smoking, social relationships will always win.

According to one study, wives who felt connected to their spouses felt less reactive toward electric shock. If one of the researchers added a caring touch as the women were subjected to the shock, the women reported lowered pain. This goes to prove the fact that empathic behaviors matter. Even children who suffered traumatic experiences at some point were found to benefit from supportive relationships in their foster homes. They bounced back to normalcy quickly.

Relationships provide trust and love. They provide a space to be encouraged and reassured, boosting mental toughness. No wonder most people run to their friends when they are in trouble. Simply put, social support from healthy relationships gives you the following benefits:

- An opportunity to express love and be loved back
- A chance to be part of something bigger than you
- An opportunity to practice social skills
- A sounding board and a place to test reality
- The benefit of other perspectives

- Networking opportunities that may have economic benefits

THE VALUE OF GOOD COMMUNICATION

No relationship, whether with a friend, a family member or a spouse, will last without affection and trust. They are the glue that holds relationships together. In a healthy relationship, people communicate these positive feelings toward each other through gestures and words. That communication ends up creating further positive communication – it is a cycle. When people in a relationship lose trust in each other, affection soon suffers and communication takes on a negative turn. They become demanding and defensive, beginning their downward spiral.

The same way relationships are vital to mental toughness is the same way good communication is vital to relationships. They all depend on each other. Good communication is also necessary for emotional resilience. It encourages positive emotions and helps people to resolve conflict better. It makes it easier to express your wants and needs authentically. Those positive emotions improve your social and physical health. They help you bond with others, creating and maintaining healthy and strong relationships. In turn, those relationships nourish your mental strength and positive feelings. It is a cyclic, self-reinforcing process. The better you feel, the more you can create relationships that make you feel better.

Bear in mind that it is the quality of your relationships, not the quantity, that determines the benefits you reap from them. People who genuinely care for you and have a connection with you are those who will provide comfort and support in times of need. Mentally tough people recognize that the best option in life isn't to "go at it alone" but instead to develop a strong community of mutual support and respect.

CHAPTER ACTIVITY: FIND SOCIAL SUPPORT

- **Nurture your friendships**

Set aside 30-60 minutes each week to catch up or share an experience with a close friend. This could be as simple as calling them and chatting on the phone or could be a planned outing to an entertainment event you'll both enjoy.

- **Use "I" statements in conflict**

When conflict arises, as it surely will, how you approach it can either escalate it or help you to resolve it. Well-resolved conflict will draw you closer to the person you are in conflict with. Make it a habit to use 'I' statements to communicate feelings instead of voicing your concerns as though they are accusations. For example, rather than 'you never text me back,' say, 'I feel hurt when you do not text me back.'

9

MONEY MENTALITY

"Money is a terrible master but an excellent servant" - **P.T. Barnum**.

A story is told of a woman who ran an egg-selling business that was always on the brink of collapse. She always had eggs but would talk to anyone who would listen about the one egg that broke, the tray that got so dirty she had to dispose of it, and how much those losses do her injustice. At one point, due to an increased cost of chicken feed, her supplier had to raise the cost of eggs. She was distraught. The move reinforced her belief that her store struggled because of a corrupt government, high costs of living, and unreasonable suppliers.

What she did not realize was that other businesses around her seemed to thrive even though the circumstances were the same. She never saw that her problems had a lot to do with how she ran her business. She would open her store late. Her presentation was never quite impressive and most of her stuff was in poor condition. Worse still, she always complained to her customers. Yet, everyone else but her was to blame for her collapsing business.

People have always asked what makes the difference between successful and unsuccessful people. In my experience as a life coach, the difference between them is their attitude. Successful people believe that they are in charge of their destiny while unsuccessful people do not. The successful set out to create their lives while the poor accept life as something that happens to them. The successful are proactive, where the unsuccessful are passive. The successful take responsibility for their future because they have an internal locus of control while the unsuccessful ones, whose locus of control is external, believe that they are victims of circumstance or fate. This chapter covers the importance of mindset when it comes to managing money and discusses the concept of internal and external loci of control, and how developing an internal sense of control can benefit you.

WHERE IS YOUR LOCUS OF CONTROL?

One of the most important characteristics of mentally strong people is the ability to overcome fear and keep moving forward despite it all. Many people have a lot of fear surrounding finances, and understandably so. According to APA's 2020 Stress in America survey, 64% of Americans report feeling stressed about money. They go about their days always concerned that they will run out of money and will not be able to take care of themselves. When they get some money, rather than using it to meet the pressing needs, they obsess that it will not be enough, and some end up misusing it.

Some people avoid looking at their finances because they associate money with pain, shame, and fear. However, this just creates more fear. Yet, when you're worried about making ends meet, every hiccup can seem near catastrophic. Conversely, when you learn to face your finances with a resilient attitude, you can develop a plan. Once you've developed a plan, those negative emotions start to fade. What once seemed impossible to manage is suddenly broken down into small, manageable steps that aren't overwhelming. Developing financial resilience along with mental toughness makes it possible to weather difficult times without giving in to despair or giving up. As with the other challenges discussed in this book, mindset is key.

We grow up conditioned to seek permission any time we want to attempt something. As a child, you need permission from your guardian to leave the table at dinner, to go play, or even to have a friend over. You need your teacher's permission to go to the bathroom. So, you grow up with the compulsion to seek permission, even when it is not necessary.

As an adult, you need permission to leave work early. You may need permission from your partner to hang out with friends first rather than mow the lawn. You need the city council's permission to build a backyard shed. You do not need permission to be you and to pursue your goals.

Yet, as a result of all the permission-seeking we do, many of us have an external locus of control. A locus of control is a psychological term describing the way you see the world around you and where you put the responsibility for the things happening in your life. If your locus of control is internal, you believe that your choices and actions determine the quality of your life. You take responsibility for who and where you are. If your locus of control is external, you believe that your environment, fate, or luck determine the quality of your life. You hold others responsible for your identity and your status in life.

It is not that you either have an external locus of control

or an internal one. It exists on a scale. Yet, many people lean on one side of the scale more than the other. This begs the question, where is your locus of control? Mentally tough people have an internal locus of control-- they accept responsibility for the things that happen to them. They realize that the only person who can fix your problems is you. These people are proactive and believe they can shape their lives. They do not give their power to others.

Having an internal locus of control is realizing that if you want something from life, it is your responsibility to get it. Of course, it takes time to shift toward an internal locus of control if yours is external, but you can learn to own your destiny and your happiness. You can learn to live a life you love. You can own your well-being. You can finally make peace with the fact that if you are unhappy, no one can ease things for you – you have to make the necessary changes yourself.

TECHNIQUES TO CULTIVATE AN INTERNAL LOCUS OF CONTROL

Shifting your locus of control internally is not just important for your happiness. It also plays a role in making your life meaningful. It is necessary for obtaining financial freedom. Financial freedom comes when you stop focusing on others, and look at your needs and situation, to work on that. It comes from dwelling only on the things that you can change. In truth, you are never free until you can let go of what you cannot control. This is not to say that change does not happen, but it happens to all men. Who you are and who you become is not shaped by the chance or misfortune that happens to you, but how you respond to it. To make it more likely that you would respond well, here are some techniques you can use:

- **Reframe blame**

Teach yourself to take responsibility for the outcome of a situation rather than shifting blame outwards. When you find yourself in trouble, how do you justify fault? What is your mindset at the time? Rather than feeling guilty or berating yourself, you can see these situations as an opportunity to improve in the future. If events are within your control, you can change them. However, if you blame other people for what happens to you, you will become reliant on others to change things. Reflect on how you can take responsibility for your finances. Are there any circumstances or situations you're currently blaming others for?

- **Take charge**

Imagine your future goals and the actions you need to take to get there. How are you framing the path forward? If you have thoughts like "if this happens, I will …" or, "I hope it goes this way" or "if I'm lucky…" you are looking at your goals through an external locus of control. You're seeing future success as dependent on someone else or some external event. You can work to change your thinking by actively challenging those types of thoughts. Instead, choose to think along the lines of "When I make this happen..." The idea is to frame them in a way that acknowledges the value of determination more than luck.

- **Embrace failure**

People with an external locus of control look at situations and assess them for the probability of failure. If they see a slight change, they will avoid the situation or choose not to try. To shift your locus of control, when you do fail, look objectively at the reasons why you failed. Was it a result of poor preparation? In what ways can you improve your own actions to help avoid this same failure in the future?

CHAPTER ACTIVITY: BECOME THE BOSS OF YOU

While riddled with challenges, recognizing that you are a free agent can be liberating. When you take things into your hands, you lay aside some fears, create your certainty and discover that you can do more than you thought possible. You become the boss of you. When it comes to your money, you need nobody's permission to buy a house, get out of debt or ask for a raise. And, no one will come from nowhere to instruct you to take out health insurance, start investing or live within your means. You have to take charge. You have to use your control to remove the money-related complications in your life and strengthen yourself. Here are a few steps to get you started:

1. **Set up an emergency fund**

Knowing that you have funds set aside to cope with minor crises and unexpected costs can help ease some of the stress and anxiety you may have around money. Start small. Set aside a few hundred dollars, then commit to gradually add to the fund as you are able.

1. **Determine what needs the most attention and make a plan**

Write down your three biggest money challenges. Once you've identified the main sources of your financial anxiety you can begin developing an action plan to manage them. Brainstorm different steps you can take to help mediate this stress. Look at both short-term and long-term approaches--what is something you can do *today* to help relieve some of your financial stress?

1. **Track your spending**

Tracking your spending can be an effective tool to develop awareness around your spending and saving practices. It can also help take some of the uncertainty and guesswork out of managing your money. Make sure that you create a budget and live by it. Ideally, a budget should have your income and expenses in separate columns to help you make sure that you live within your means. Design your budget with your goals in mind. For example, if you want to get out of debt, set aside a specific amount of money that you pay every month toward offsetting your debt, and make that a priority.

10

BE IN THE BUSINESS OF SUCCESS

"Success is not final; failure is not fatal: It is the courage to continue that counts." - **Winston Churchill.**

Remember the woman with the challenging egg business in Chapter 9? Running a business can be fun and exciting until you run into obstacles. Like her, many people get in, hoping that they will succeed and gain some degree of status, but without a full picture of the challenges, they will have to overcome to get there.

In business, having smooth sailing operations is a myth. Running a business is a lot like putting out fires one after the other. Sometimes the fire will burn down something of value and you will have to build back up. Other times the fire will burn hubris and you will survive it as a more accomplished business person. Whatever the case, you have to be prepared to meet obstacles and have to brace yourself for them so that you can overcome them.

When I was about ten years old, a classmate, Billy, broke his arm at the beginning of the summer art class. He was disappointed because he really wanted to be part of the intensive art class where we met and spent the whole day being creative. He went to our teacher, showed her his cast and expressed his disappointment that he couldn't participate.

'Why can't you participate?' asked Mrs. Whitecotton. 'People with disabilities make art.'

'But I can't use my hands!' exclaimed Billy.

Mrs. Whitecotton went on to explain to us that disability is not inability. She introduced us to artists with disabilities - how they strapped paintbrushes to their wheelchairs or used their mouths to paint. She helped Billy to paint with his mouth and his feet. Watching them all through, I learned an important lesson that has kept me in my life coach and running my business as a fitness instructor, before. The lesson? That you just have to find a different way to do what you want to do.

Over the years, that lesson has looked different. At one point, my main concern was; how do I keep my business engaged without sufficient funds? How do we keep operating? The solution? Find a different way. In that case, the different way was to compartmentalize the pain of a tight budget and work with the long-term goal in mind. At another point, my biggest problem was working around many commitments and the solution principle was still the same. Find another way - and here, I hired an assistant.

Business is like that. If you will succeed, you have to be committed to the principles, and open to the fact that challenges must come. In this chapter, you will find solutions to some of the challenges you face as a business owner and worker. You will learn strategies that will help you to overcome difficulties or avoid them altogether.

BE YOUR OWN CHAMPION

Everyone experiences challenges with work and business, but how you handle them determines whether you're able to bounce back and continue to grow. Many obstacles that seem unavoidable can actually be attributed to mismanaged emotions, detrimental habits, and interpersonal missteps. Mental toughness can help you overcome obstacles and challenging business situations. It will help you to cheer yourself on. To succeed in business, you have to be your own champion. You need to believe that you're capable of overcoming challenges and adapting to change.

Mental toughness allows you to listen to your gut when it comes to business decisions surrounding people and work. We all have an inbuilt radar that lets us know when a mistake is lurking around the corner – we can identify beforehand people who will prove troublesome. Yet, most people choose to ignore the signal. According to research, that is one of the major reasons businesses fail. It contributes to managerial incompetence.

Mental toughness will help you to choose the right people. It will allow you to trust your assessment of interviewees and to keep doing interviews until you have the right fit for your business. It will allow you to sidestep the trap many business people fall into – that of choosing employees solely based on friendship, rather than accomplishment. In the excitement of onboarding someone, they ignore their gut feeling. Eventually, they open their business up to incompetence. Mental toughness will allow you to overcome the obstacles to your business success. It will help you to implement strategies that guarantee your excellence.

STRATEGIES FOR OVERCOMING BUSINESS OBSTACLES

- **Be willing to abandon what doesn't work**

Rather than clinging to products, services, or strategies that aren't working, successful people are able to recognize when to redirect their efforts elsewhere. They are able to evaluate what doesn't work and use that information to improve upon their business, and you can do the same too. We tend to get smitten with our products. We grow attached to how we do business and find it hard to make adjustments. It is almost as if that creates blinders for us so that we never see things that may be clear to an outsider. If you are going to succeed in business, you have to be willing to fold. You have to be willing to let go when the time is right. Cultivate the courage to walk away before a product or service becomes a major obstacle and you waste energy that you could direct elsewhere solving what should not have been a problem in the first place.

- **Replace old strategies with new ones**

People often cling to old ways of doing business because that's what they're comfortable with. Don't let yourself become so set in your ways that you're unable to evolve - you should constantly be reviewing and assessing your business strategies and looking for ways to continue leveling up. As a rule of thumb, when you abandon an old strategy, if it was vital to how you do business, replace it with another one that works better. Watch out for strategies that you need, only improve rather than throw out entirely.

- **Plan in advance**

While it's important to prioritize immediate objectives and deal with issues as they arise, mentally tough people recognize that you need to plan ahead in order to make the most of opportunities and manage challenges as they arise. When you're constantly reacting to events, you miss the opportunity for long-term strategy development. Make sure that you come up with an execution plan for the different departments in your business. In fact, if you can, plan around anticipated failures.

CHAPTER ACTIVITY: EXIST TO EXCEL

- **Seek out critiques**

Mentally tough people recognize that feedback is an important part of the course-correcting process, and is to be sought out rather than avoided. Make a habit of seeking feedback from peers, bosses, and people who report to you. By getting input from a variety of sources you can develop a better, more realistic picture of how you're doing.

- **Brainstorm solutions**

Make a list of the biggest business challenges that you're currently facing, and come up with ten possible solutions for each one. You might think that ten is too many, but the goal of this exercise is to get you to think outside the box and come up with new perspectives and strategies.

- **Design your long-term plan**

Set aside time this week to develop a long-term plan for your business or job. Where do you want to be a year from now? What will be different, and what goals are you setting?

- **Create a schedule**

Choose one day of the week that you will use as a planning day - many people find that Sundays are a good time to look at the week ahead. At the beginning of each month, make a plan. Choose your top three goals for the month and outline how you'll measure your progress and what the desired outcome is. Then, each week, on the designated day, sit down and make a weekly plan. Decide what projects and tasks you'll focus on that week that relates to each of your goals. Note any commitments or potential obstacles that might arise, and come up with a plan for how you'll manage them. Block out time in your calendar and be realistic about your availability and the time required for each task. At the beginning of each day, review your weekly tasks and choose small, specific things to do to make progress towards completing your major goals.

11

QUIETING YOUR INNER CRITIC

"Do one thing every day that scares you." - **Eleanor Roosevelt.**

There is an old story about a baby elephant tied to a post. As he pulls and tags on the rope, it will not budge. The rope is too strong for him and so is the post. He keeps trying until eventually, he resigns himself to his fate. He accepts the fact that he is stuck there. Eventually, he grows and becomes an adult with a huge tusk, giant legs and a swirly trunk that can break the post and rope almost effortlessly. But, at this point, the elephant believes that the rock and the post are immovable and so he stays there, falsely believing that he could never leave.

The story of this elephant mirrors the story of many people. They walk around life and find it easy to blame others or external situations for their inability to reach their goals. Think about it, what is your immediate thought when you fall short of your targets? Who do you blame? Have you ever considered that you might be the one holding yourself back, possibly limiting yourself because of the things you have come to hold as true? We have beliefs about all sorts of things and these beliefs influence the things we do and whether or not we are good at them.

When our beliefs are empowering, they charge us and make our achievements seem effortless. If our beliefs are limiting, it feels like we are pushing against an impossible wall. Limiting beliefs are difficult to spot. They creep on us, make a home in our hearts and then show up in different ways when we least expect them, getting in the way of what we truly want to do. They make life harder and wear out our mental toughness. Think about it; if your beliefs influence your results, how much more powerful would you be if you could believe things that empower, sustain, nurture and support you?

That is the essence of this chapter. Here, you will learn how to challenge and prevent self-pity and self-blame. You will become aware of the beliefs you have come to live by and be equipped to recognize those that limit you. Even if you only implement one of the simple tips that will be provided later in this chapter, you will have taken a major step toward freeing yourself of self-pity and self-blame. You will be on the right path toward being mentally tough. The mentally tough do not cave into self-blame and self-pity. They challenge the nagging voices in their heads and rise above them.

UNDERSTANDING SELF-LIMITING BELIEFS

A belief is a feeling of certainty regarding the meaning you attach to something. If a belief is limiting, then it prevents you from pursuing the things you desire. It stops you from applying for a promotion, leaving a toxic relationship, standing up for yourself when you are being taken advantage of, and generally going after your goals. A self-limiting belief puts limitations and boundaries on the things you see to be reasonable. It holds you back from the person you would like to be. Like the elephant, you stay stuck to a post that has no power over you, without even being aware of it.

Bear in mind that you typically feel convinced that your belief is correct unless you question it. The reason you feel so certain is that you have told yourself that same story all your life, unconsciously looking for evidence that it is true. You have found a lot of proof towards it because you were looking for it. In the case of the elephant, when he was little, he pulled and tugged on the post long enough and hard enough to be convinced that he could not prevail. Every time his attempts failed, he found proof that the rope and the post were his destiny. In the same way, you create more limitations as you look for proof that your limiting belief is true.

Self-limiting beliefs also include the things you believe about the world around you, not just what you believe about yourself. To use the elephant analogy one last time, the adult elephant has come to believe that he is not strong enough to move the post. He also believes that the rope and the post are immovable. Can you identify his limiting beliefs? Simply put, limiting beliefs can be divided into three categories:

Common limiting beliefs

1. **Limiting beliefs about yourself**

Limiting beliefs about you create the illusion that you cannot do something because you are naturally troubled. They are the most impactful because they convince you that whatever is wrong, is inherent. For example, someone who could write well might believe that they are by nature a bad writer because they got a poor grade or two when writing in school. Nothing holds you back in life like having this kind of belief because it often comes with insecurities, baggage, and emotional attachments that you have to unravel if you will change the belief.

Many people, for example, use age as a crutch so that they never really attempt things they want to do. They claim they are too old to date, learn a new skill, or even change careers. Alternatively, they imagine themselves to be too young to move to a new city, apply for a job they want, or pursue a certain career. Limiting beliefs about yourself could also touch on your personality traits. It could be that you imagine yourself to be dumb because you could not start conversations at a young age – a factor of your personality. The tricky part about limiting beliefs based on personality quirks is that sometimes you cannot change them.

Then, there is the issue of feelings. You may not know this, but your emotions are the basis for your limiting beliefs about yourself. For example, you may believe that you are too depressed for anyone to like you, and so you start to accept that you cannot meet new people. When you do something embarrassing at work, you quit because you cannot believe that anyone could believe it was not intentional. Paradoxically, the things you need to do to deal with these emotions are the same things the limiting beliefs trick you out of doing.

If you are depressed, for example, socializing will help deal with the sadness. If you are embarrassed, facing other people's judgment will help you get over it, and so forth. Limiting beliefs cheat you out of doing these things, creating a vicious cycle. You end up proving your wrong assumptions to yourself.

1. **Limiting beliefs about the world**

When I was younger, I thought that anyone who talked to me did so because they wanted something from me. I couldn't imagine a world where people talked to you simply because they liked to. I am not sure where the idea came from, but it is an example of a limiting belief about the world. It prevented me from trusting others, which meant that I was lonely for a long time. We develop limiting beliefs about the world from disapproval – what other people will allow or not allow us to do. For example, you might fear talking to people because you assume they will think you are weird.

In relationships, couples might fear pursuing their individual goals because they do not want to disappoint each other. You might avoid leaving a low-paying but a noble job for fear that people would lose their respect for you. As a rule of thumb, if you are considering an issue and the first thought you have is 'what will others think?' you have already lost. For starters, people do not care that much, and secondly, they are too busy worrying over their own issues to worry about you. Besides, what is the worst that can happen if they do not approve of you? You get to live your life on your own terms.

Other than disapproval, prejudice could also cause you to have some limiting beliefs about the world. Sadly, the world is not free of discrimination. People are still sexist and racist. It is easy to be defined by such people if you are not careful so that you think things like: 'I am Asian, and women dislike Asian men, so I will always be alone.' One way to think about prejudices is to remind yourself that even though they could seem true in one scenario, they are not true for everyone.

A final source of limiting beliefs about the world could be illusions of grandeur. While all other examples I have provided so far have to do with casting yourself in your own story negatively, this one is different. If you have illusions of grandeur, you imagine yourself special – so special, that the world cannot handle you. For example, an artist might think;

'I would like to sing, but no one appreciates my eclectic taste.' Of course, this is a twisted type of entitlement where you imagine the world to owe you because you are very special, but it does not understand your uniqueness so you never try.

1. **Limiting beliefs about life**

Sometimes, how you think your life ought to play out can be a limiting belief. For example, you imagine that you are too old to start a new business. The assumption here is that your time has already passed, so why even try. Most of our limiting beliefs about life revolve around time. You assume that there is not enough of it left for you to try. Someone wanting to change their diet might say they are too busy to eat home-cooked meals. The excuse ends up hiding the fact that they have not prioritized changing their diet.

Limiting beliefs about life causes you to fall into a little safe routine and to hide behind an outward identity. You spend your time on distractions, afraid that you would rock the boat. Of course, this comes with another assumption that whatever you want, does not even exist. For example, you might say to yourself when you fail to change your diet, that a perfectly healthy person does not exist. You end up believing that going on a diet is impossible, which prevents you from trying.

It is clear that self-limiting beliefs are deep-seated beliefs you have about yourself and the world around you that hold you back. They are the stories we've told ourselves our entire lives, and that our minds are constantly looking to sustain. It is also true that while self-limiting beliefs can hold you back from realizing your true potential, they can be changed, and you can harness your mental toughness to create this change. Imagine how much you could accomplish if your beliefs actively sustained and nurtured you rather than tearing you down.

Reflection: *Think about the following statements and try to complete them with the first thing that comes to mind. It will help you to identify some of your self-limiting beliefs:*

- I don't have time to …
- I can't… because I am not…
- I am not good enough to …
- I will be judged if I …
- I'm not as good as … in
- I'm a failure because I …
- I can never …

CHAPTER ACTIVITY: DISMANTLING LIMITING BELIEFS

- **Practice positive self-talk**

This step requires you to follow one simple rule: don't say anything to yourself that you wouldn't say to someone else. The idea is to practice being actively encouraging with yourself and challenge any negative thoughts as they arise. Make a list of affirmations that you can refer to when you are struggling with negative thinking.

- **Do not ruminate on the negative**

The next time you have a negative experience, try to reduce the amount of time you dwell on the situation. Set aside a time block for yourself to think about the experience, and at the end of that time commit to moving forward. Do not linger on the topic. If the temptation arises, remind yourself that you're only human and are allowed to make mistakes.

- **Find positive distractions**

Sometimes the best thing you can do to get out of your own head is to focus on a distraction. Only ensure that the distraction is serving you well. Make a list of activities and hobbies that you can engage in when you feel yourself sinking into a negative headspace.

- **Challenge limiting beliefs**

First, write down any limiting belief that you observe in yourself. Acknowledge that it is just a belief, not the truth. Write down a new belief that challenges the old story you've been telling yourself and commit to acting as if your new belief is true for the next week. Do this for long enough and you will change how you think.

12

PERSEVERING DESPITE IT ALL

"A bend in the road is not the end of the road... unless you fail to make the turn." - **Helen Keller.**

Everyone gets them – those feelings of fear, doubt, insecurity, and a lack of self-assurance. Whatever we set out to achieve, no matter how determined we are, there always comes a time when the challenges ahead of us seem overwhelming. Our motivation dwindles and we feel like throwing our hands up in the air, in surrender. During those periods, when someone says to you that 'giving up is not an option', you feel grossly misunderstood. How could they say that without really knowing how many obstacles you are facing? You wonder. You realize that your biggest question at the time is how not to quit.

In the gym, whenever someone has been working hard for ages and they can barely see results, they become discouraged. I had one client years ago – she really wanted to have well-chiseled abs and so she put in the work. Every day, like clockwork, she showed up to the gym and worked herself to exhaustion. Then, she took a sip of water and pushed herself some more. She was always asking about eating well, careful that a plate does not undo all her hard work. After three months of faithfulness, she looked in the mirror and saw nothing. There was not even a hint of muscle on her stomach.

When she came to me the next day, she wanted to give up. She was done trying to achieve the impossible, she said. I encouraged her to keep going. On a bluff, I asked her to do her workout program faithfully for one more month and if she still saw no results, she could give up with my blessing. I was buying time to figure out how to motivate her, but it turned out that my advice was spot on. In less than two weeks, her abs shaped up nicely. She was so proud of herself that she did not give up when the night seemed darkest.

In this chapter, you will learn how to keep going even during the tough times. You will learn how to persevere, despite the overwhelming feeling of wanting just to give up. You will realize that the power lies in your mindset and changing it will keep you motivated to persevere when the going gets tough. The Merriam-Webster dictionary defines perseverance as the "continued effort to do or achieve something despite difficulties, failure, or opposition." Perseverance is what makes the difference between success and failure at the end of the day. Like consistency, it's an essential quality for the mentally tough individual. Here, you will see how to challenge self-doubt and limiting beliefs and persevere in the face of obstacles.

GETTING BACK ON TRACK AFTER A SLIP-UP

So, you've taken action to start creating real change in your life. You've been completing your exercises and action steps, and are making progress. Then, something comes along that stops you in your tracks. You start to feel overwhelmed again and fall out of some of the new habits you've been practicing. The first thing you need to know is that: it's okay. Like change and adversity, slipping up is normal. This is when you get to really put your new attitude and mindset into practice - when things aren't going your way. Our brains are designed to give up easily and want an immediate reward, so it can be discouraging when we experience failure and setbacks. It starts to seem as though giving up is your best option because:

- **You mistake lessons for failure**

Being mentally tough is learning to see setbacks as lessons. If you do not see roadblocks as opportunities to learn, then you will not keep going. You will start to think that the outcome is more important than the progress and that will further steal your motivation and dissuade you from trying again.

- **You predict failure before it happens**

Another reason you may feel the strong urge to give up is lacking the optimism that you will succeed. You start to expect that no matter what you do, you will fail. This is a form of self-sabotage. Self-sabotaging in this way is about creating a thought that success is impossible for you.

- **You lack discipline**

It could also be that you are demotivated because you do not have the discipline to keep showing up. Discipline comes from the realization that the things you want will not just happen to you in a few weeks. It takes determination and hard work to actually succeed.

- **You are not adjusting to change**

If you do not adjust to change, you will certainly cave to the temptation to give up. Change happens to everyone, everywhere. The mentally tough know how to embrace it. They know how to tweak their ideas and find ways to evolve. They can easily accept things even when they do not play out as imagined.

BURSTING THE MYTH OF INSTANT SUCCESS

Of course, another reason you may not persevere is disappointment that you are not achieving your goals as fast as you hoped you would. Instant success is a myth that convinces us that everyone else is getting what they want without needing to put in the same effort as us. This is especially true in today's generation where instant gratification is hailed. It creates an illusion that everyone has all they want. When you scroll through your social media feed, you are tempted to think that people achieved their success overnight.

The truth though, is that anyone who has ever been successful, legitimately so, has put in the work. They had to deal with a lot of failure on their journey. To be mentally tough is to remind yourself that even though you are not privy to the struggles of others as they got to the top, you can trust that they did struggle. That way, you remind yourself that the destination is not all the story there is to the success. Understanding this myth, you stay undeterred by your setbacks. You realize that the real magic happens during the journey, and the memories and experiences along the way are what you eventually learn from.

Don't quit too soon

As it is, many people often give up when they are in

reality close to success. Imagine if the lady I told you about had actually quit. How would she have handled the realization that if she had kept trying, she would have succeeded? In life, the toughest times are often the step right before a major breakthrough. They had it right when they said that 'it is darkest before dawn.' Think of it as a sort of test that you must pass to prove that what you are working toward is exactly what you want.

To keep going is to choose to believe in yourself. It is to say that despite all evidence to the contrary, and against all odds, you place your bet on your future, as a successful person. It is to stake your life on your goals and trust that everything will work out. It is trusting the process. Do not give up on your future self and risk becoming regretful because you quit too soon.

CHAPTER ACTIVITY: BATTLING THE DESIRE TO QUIT

- **Remember your "why"**

Think back to the motivation behind your actions - what is your reason for wanting to persist? Why did you begin pursuing your goal? Put yourself back into the mental space you were in when you felt inspired and excited to take action. This helps you refocus on the purpose behind your actions.

- **Visualize the end result**

Before you can achieve a goal, you need to know what it actually looks like. That is where visualization comes in. It helps you see the goal to believe it. It is a technique where you create a mental picture of your goal. When you visualize the outcome you desire, you start seeing it as a real possibility. It works because your brain interprets imagery the same way it would interpret real-life action. When tempted to give up, imagine yourself having achieved your goal. What would your life look like? Write down the specific details that would change. Create an elaborate mental image and add as many details as you can.

- **Celebrate your small victories**

Write out a list of accomplishments you've already completed, regardless of how small they may seem. Continue adding to this list as you complete other tasks and achieve victories, and refer back to it when you're feeling discouraged.

- **Do a "brain dump"**

Take a pen and paper and create three columns. In the first columns write your musts -things you've committed to doing. Write your wants in the second column and in the third column, write the things that you may perhaps do. Evaluate each list and eliminate unnecessary tasks. It will help to relieve your brain of extra baggage and allow you to focus on what is important to you.

CONCLUSION

One of the most potent and sacred rituals to live your life mindfully, consciously, and authentically is to take charge of your mind. It is to have your heart and mind united toward one goal and watch the dormant person inside you come to life. It's to create powerful and strong boundaries with yourself so that you can put forward your best version. This is the essence of mental toughness as has been discussed in this book. The mentally tough know themselves. They have learned their pre-programmed responses and learned how to make choices that are true to who they are. They rely on habits – good mental habits to keep going. They are masters of their minds, controlling their thoughts, rather than being controlled by their thoughts.

Your mind is the surest tool you have to succeed in life. It is your most powerful tool to create good in your life. More specifically, your thoughts affect your perception and how you interpret reality. According to research, the average person has about 70,000 thoughts every day. That's crazy to think about. Imagine if a majority of those thoughts are self-abusive, unproductive, or simply a waste of energy. They can

CONCLUSION

ruin your life. In this book, you have learned the key to taking back your power from your mind – mental toughness. You have seen why it is important to take control of your mind – to be someone who is actively and consciously thinking your thoughts.

You know that mental strength is a muscle that must be exercised, like other muscles in the body, it will grow. You have interacted with the characteristics of the mentally strong and so you know what you are aspiring towards. I set out to help you understand mental toughness in the most persuasive way I could think of. I laid out my journey and my life. I coupled that up with research and the strength of personal experience. The goal? - To make sure that you have no excuse. You know the role mindset plays in your response to challenges, you recognize why everything you do on a daily basis matters and how your habits stick.

You recognize the inevitability of change, the place of emotions, and the need to ride the emotional wave as you adapt to change. You can see why the relationships you keep, the people you hang around, matter. You already have everything you need to persevere, so do not let yourself get in your way for another day. Your first step toward living the kind of life you have always wanted begins here, today, now. The question is, will you take it?

A SHORT MESSAGE FROM THE AUTHOR

Hey, are you enjoying the book? I'd love to hear your thoughts!

Many readers do not know how hard reviews are to come by, and how much they help an author.

I would be incredibly grateful if you could take just few seconds to write a brief review on Amazon, even if it's just a few sentences!

Thank you for taking the time to share your thoughts!
Your review will genuinely make a difference for me and help gain exposure for my work.

Jed Wood

SPECIAL OFFER

Special Bonus!
Want This Bonus Book For Free?

Get **FREE**, unlimited access to it and all of my new books by joining the Fan Base!

  Scan With Your Phone Camera To Join!

REFERENCES

4 Tips for Keeping a Gratitude Journal. (2020, September 23). Cleveland Clinic. https://health.clevelandclinic.org/tips-for-keeping-a-gratitude-journal/

adversity. (n.d.). The Merriam-Webster.Com Dictionary. Retrieved September 15, 2021, from https://www.merriam-webster.com/dictionary/adversity

Asplund, B. J. (2021, June 4). *When Americans Use Their Strengths More, They Stress Less*. Gallup.Com.

Cherry, K. (2021, July 16). *The Best Ways to Cultivate Your Mental Strength*. Verywell Fit. https://www.verywellfit.com/how-to-cultivate-mental-toughness-4134660

Clear, J. (2020a, February 4). *Identity-Based Habits: How to Actually Stick to Your Goals This Year*. James Clear. https://jamesclear.com/identity-based-habits

Clear, J. (2020b, February 4). *The Science of Developing Mental Toughness in Health, Work, and Life*. James Clear. https://jamesclear.com/mental-toughness

Ewing, T. (2020, August 12). *5 Habits Of Mentally Strong People—Based On Science*. Forbes. https://www.forbes.-

com/sites/tonyewing/2020/07/24/5-habits-of-mentally-strong-people-based-on-science/?sh=782bb0e37a33

Gallup, Inc. (2012, January 23). *FAQ: Defining Talents and Strengths*. Gallup.Com. https://www.strengthsquest.com/help/general/143096/difference-talent-strength.aspx

Gleeson, B. (2020, July 7). *13 Habits Of Mentally Tough People*. Forbes. https://www.forbes.com/sites/brentgleeson/2020/06/24/13-habits-of-mentally-tough-people/?sh=344bb8545d4d

Gratitude Journal (Greater Good in Action). (n.d.). Berkeley.Edu. Retrieved September 15, 2021, from https://ggia.berkeley.edu/practice/gratitude_journal

Itani, O. (2021, February 9). *12 Habits That Will Help You Build Real Grit and Mental Strength*. OMAR ITANI. https://www.omaritani.com/blog/12-habits-mental-strength

Lin, Y. (2017). *Mental Toughness and Individual Differences in Learning, Educational and Work Performance, Psychological Well-being, and Personality: A Systematic Review*. Frontiers. https://www.frontiersin.org/articles/10.3389/fpsyg.2017.01345/full

More than just a cue, intrinsic reward helps make exercise a habit. (n.d.). ScienceDaily. Retrieved September 15, 2021, from https://www.sciencedaily.com/releases/2016/09/160913101129.htm

The Neuroscience Behind Habit Change. (2020, February 11). Forbes. https://www.forbes.com/sites/ellevate/2020/02/11/the-neuroscience-behind-habit-change/?sh=3a56e01b6f6a

Power, R. (2021, January 5). *5 Ways to Embrace Change at Work and in Life*. Inc.Com. https://www.inc.com/rhett-power/5-ways-to-embrace-change-at-work-and-in-life.html

The Reason Why You're Struggling to Be Consistent (And How to Fix It). (2020, September 26). Spiritual Living For Busy

REFERENCES

People. https://www.spirituallivingforbusypeople.com/consistent

Ribeiro, M. B. (2021, April 15). *How to Become Mentally Strong: 14 Strategies for Building Resilience*. PositivePsychology.Com. https://positivepsychology.com/mentally-strong/

The Science Behind Adopting New Habits (And Making Them Stick). (2021, June 29). Forbes. https://www.forbes.com/sites/quora/2018/02/13/the-science-behind-adopting-new-habits-and-making-them-stick/?sh=175f31c643c7

Scott, E. (2020a, February 25). *How to Reduce Negative Self-Talk for a Better Life*. Verywell Mind. https://www.verywellmind.com/negative-self-talk-and-how-it-affects-us-4161304

Scott, E. (2020b, November 24). *How Cognitive Distortions Can Fuel Your Stress*. Verywell Mind. https://www.verywellmind.com/cognitive-distortions-and-stress-3144921

Sparks, D. (2019, May 29). *Mayo Mindfulness: Overcoming negative self-talk*. Https://Newsnetwork.Mayoclinic.Org/. https://newsnetwork.mayoclinic.org/discussion/mayo-mindfulness-overcoming-negative-self-talk/

Spiney, K. (2021, July 25). *The Importance of Believing in Yourself (Even When You Don't)*. Katherine Spinney Coaching. https://www.katherinespinney.com/importance-of-believing-in-yourself/

Suttie, J. (2017, November 13). *Four Ways Social Support Makes You More Resilient*. Greater Good. https://greatergood.berkeley.edu/article/item/four_ways_social_support_makes_you_more_resilient

Tasler, N. (2017, April 5). *How to Get Better at Dealing with Change*. Harvard Business Review. https://hbr.org/2016/09/how-to-get-better-at-dealing-with-change

Taylor, C. G. (2020, July 6). *The power of reframing what we mean by "personal strengths" at work*. Future Talent Learning.

REFERENCES

https://www.futuretalentlearning.com/en/future-talent-learning-blog/the-power-of-reframing-what-we-mean-by-personal-strengths-at-work

Team, B. A. S. (2020, October 2). *How to Turn Your Negative Thinking Around*. Cleveland Clinic. https://health.clevelandclinic.org/turn-around-negative-thinking/

Thelwell, R., Weston, N., & Greenlees, I. (2005). Defining and Understanding Mental Toughness within Soccer. *Journal of Applied Sport Psychology, 17*(4), 326–332. https://doi.org/10.1080/10413200500313636

White, D. L. M. (2016, May 17). *Challenging Our Cognitive Distortions and Creating Positive Outlooks*. Psych Central. https://psychcentral.com/lib/challenging-our-cognitive-distortions-and-creating-positive-outlooks#1

Wignall, N. (2020, October 22). *10 Types of Negative Self-Talk (and How to Correct Them)*. Nick Wignall. https://nickwignall.com/negative-self-talk/

Made in the USA
Columbia, SC
19 November 2021

49346956R00071